GARLAND STUDIES ON

THE ELDERLY IN AMERICA

edited by

STUART BRUCHEY
ALLAN NEVINS PROFESSOR EMERITUS
COLUMBIA UNIVERSITY

A GARLAND SERIES

THE ASIAN INDIAN ELDERLY IN AMERICA

An Examination of Values, Family, and Life Satisfaction

JYOTSNA MIRLE KALAVAR

GARLAND PUBLISHING, Inc.
A MEMBER OF THE TAYLOR & FRANCIS GROUP
NEW YORK & LONDON / 1998

Library of Congress Cataloging-in-Publication Data

Kalavar, Jyotsna Mirle, 1963–
    The Asian Indian elderly in America
        p.   cm. — (Garland studies on the elderly in America)
    Includes bibliographical references and index.
    ISBN 0-8153-3021-9 (alk. paper)
        1. East Indian Americans—Social conditions. 2. Asian
American aged—Social conditions. 3. Quality of life—United
States. 4. Satisfaction. I. Series.
E184.E2K35 1998
305.26'08995073—dc21

                                                    98-15138

Printed on acid-free, 250-year-life paper
Manufactured in the United States of America

Dedication

To my Gurus,

Sri Sri Sri Abhinava Vidyatirtha Mahaswamigalu

& Sri Sri Sri Bharathi Tirtha Mahaswamigalu

of Sri Sharada Peetham, Sringeri (India)

Table of Contents

List of Tables

Preface

The experience of aging can differ tremendously in different cultures and subcultural groups. Resettlement from one culture to another in late life can be exacting, and demand considerable adjustment. Although, there is substantial literature on the problem of immigrants, the issues faced by older immigrants have been for the most part neglected. Very little is known about older immigrants, and especially how they live on a day to day basis. Demographics suggest that Asians are the fastest growing immigrants to the United States. Perhaps, because of their recent arrival, or the assumption that Asians take care of their own, nominal attention has been paid to immigrant Asian elderly.

Acknowledging the diversity among older Asians, this book focuses on immigrant Asian Indian elderly in the United States. Based on extensive interviews with fifty older Asian Indian immigrants, this book depicts their background, lifestyle, life satisfaction, and perceptions of life in the United States. A notable portion of the fieldwork was conducted between 1989-1990. Being an "insider" to the community, some of the advantages of access, trust, and understanding the subtleties of Indian culture accrued to the project. The older individuals described are fairly representative of those who relocate in late life. As a result, numerous South Asians may be able to identify with the narratives presented.

January 1998
Jyotsna (Josi) M. Kalavar, Ph.D.

Acknowledgements

The initiation and completion of my doctoral work would not have been possible without the prayers, encouragement, and assistance from family, teachers, and friends. I am grateful to my parents, Sharadamba and Mirle Subbarao Krishnaswamy for their enthusiasm, support, and the impetus they provided to begin graduate work in the United States. My dear husband, Gopinath, provided me with strength, motivation, and relentless patience that enabled me to complete this book. And finally, my darling sons, Abhinav and Samir, who make life exciting. Their refreshing perspective of the world has kept me entertained throughout this endeavor.

The Asian Indian Elderly
in America

I

Introduction

America has absorbed many sizeable waves of immigrants from different parts of the world. As a direct result of the elimination of national origin quotas in 1965, Asians have been settling in the United States at an unprecedented rate over the past three decades. According to Immigration and Naturalization Services statistics for Fiscal Year 1986 (United States Bureau of the Census, 1989), persons from Asian countries and the Pacific islands accounted for close to half of all the immigrants entering the United States. And this trend is expected to continue.

In recent years, gerontologists have taken note of the tremendous diversity in the American population over age sixty. Asian American elderly are the fastest growing older minority population in U.S.A. In 1980, Asian immigrants age 60 and over comprised 322,000 individuals; that figure had doubled by 1990 to 671,000 persons age 60 and over of Asian ancestry (United States Bureau of the Census, 1993). Overall, the foreign-born population has a higher proportion of people aged 65 years and over than does the native-born population (U.S. Bureau of the Census, 1981). Census data suggest that in 1995, there were about 1.1 million elderly legal immigrants. Nearly one-third of these older immigrants are from Asia or the Pacific Islands.

The label "Asian American" is both misleading and meaningless, as it does not capture the diversity that exists among members of various groups classified under this rubric. In the totality of American perception, all Asians are treated as one group, devoid of cultural and ethnic differences (Lee, 1991). In reality, they are a diverse group of people from countries in East Asia, South Asia, Southeast Asia and the Pacific Islands, with varying linguistic, religious, and lifestyle characteristics.

ASIAN INDIANS IN THE UNITED STATES

Unlike the Chinese and Japanese immigrants who came to the United States in large numbers as early as the mid to late 1800's, Asian Indians have largely arrived on American shores during the past twenty-five years (Melendy, 1977). From 1980 to 1990, the population of Asian Indians increased by 125.6% (United States Bureau of the Census, 1991). According to the 1990 census, there were 815,447 Asian Indians in the United States, making it the fourth-largest Asian American group. Asian Indians have become significant and major contributors to the "new" flow of immigrants coming to America.

Asian Indians have been visible beneficiaries of the preference provision of the 1965 Immigration Act, which gave priority to the reunification of families. This has largely resulted in chain migration of Asian Indian families. As young immigrants arrived, anchored their roots, acquired permanent residency or citizenship of the United States, they brought eligible relatives into the country. These early immigrants "paved the way" for other family members. This phenomenal growth of Asian Indians in the United States is intricately linked to the history of immigration policy for Asians.

The occupational profiles of Asian Indians in the United States reflect their high educational attainments. According to Sheth (1995), Asian Indians are more highly represented in professional occupations than any other immigrant group. By virtue of their high educational levels, Asian Indians as a group earn substantially higher family incomes than the national average. In additional to their high educational achievements, Asian Indian immigrants do not have serious language barriers, and thus have been more successful in maintaining their preimmigrant professional occupations than other Asian immigrants maintain. Also, a large number of Asian Indians have adjusted their status to permanent residents after completing their graduate programs in the United States. According to the United States Bureau of the Census (1990), Asian Indian immigrants admitted prior to 1980 were characterized by high educational levels; 71% held a Bachelor's degree, and 45% held a Master's degree. However, there has been a substantial drop in Asian Indian immigrants' educational level – only 22% of the 1985-1990 immigrants held a Master's degree. The drastic decline in the number of professional immigrants and increase in immigration based on family reunification have explained this change.

Asian Indians are the most scattered group in terms of geographic distribution in the United States. They are more evenly distributed throughout the United States than most other Asian groups. According to the United States Bureau of the Census (1990), 32% of Asian Indians reside in the Northeast and Mid-Atlantic region, followed by 26% in the South, and 24% in the West. The settlement patterns of Asian Indians in the United States reflect the absence of a territorial community (Sheth, 1995). Asian Indians have also largely refrained from living in ethnic enclaves in the United States.

Elderly Asian Indian immigrants

According to Sheth (1995), the Asian Indian population doubled in the 1980s, and grew tenfold between the years 1970 and 1990. More than 10% more parents of immigrants from India immigrated in 1988 as compared to 1982. The changing age distribution of the population is evident from current population surveys conducted between 1979 and 1988 that revealed an increase in the older age group. Although the largest age group among immigrant Asian Indians remains the 25-44 group, the 45 and above age group has seen a consistent increase from about 12% in 1979 to nearly 29% in 1988 (U.S. Bureau of the Census, 1993). Undoubtedly, Asian Indian elderly are a rapidly growing cultural minority in the United States.

Despite changing demographics, very little is known about Asian Indian elders in the United States. Culture shock, role reversal, and adapting to a new society are big thresholds for older immigrants to cross. Perhaps because of their recent arrival or the media blitz about Asians being the "model minority," or the assumption that Asians take care of their own, scant attention has been paid to the issues of older Asian immigrants. The "model minority" image is only the partial truth and obscures many deep seated problems in the Asian American community. It trivializes the social and mental health problems facing Asian Americans either by implying there are no such problems or by suggesting that Asian Americans can handle these problems on their own (Liu et al, 1990).

Researchers have pointed out that we know very little about specific ethnic groups (New, Henderson & Padgett, 1985; Jackson, 1989), much less the old who are immigrants in this country, and especially about how they live on a day-to-day basis. Older adults must make multiple adjustments in areas like language, living arrangement, communication style, dress, food habits, social outlook, finance, interpersonal relations, health care, housing, and basic life-style. The question then is—how are these older adults faring? Gibson (1989) stressed the importance of research on aging minority populations for two good reasons—to increase the core body of knowledge regarding minority aging, and to see how research questions regarding minority aging articulate with the larger body of gerontological knowledge. Since very little research on immigrant Asian Indian elderly is available; this book provides insights into their lives in the United States.

CULTURAL DIFFERENCES

In late life, moving from an Eastern culture like India to a Western society, such as the United States may be a traumatic experience. For the old, who have spent a substantial portion of their lives in their native homeland, and have maintained familial roles and social networks in accordance with Indian traditions, a move from India to the

United States may be especially critical and stressful. As Tsukahira (1988) stated, older immigrants and refugees from Asia & the Pacific Islands commonly suffer from culture shock and loneliness. Kuo and Tsai (1986) reported the usage of "uprooting" as a term in several studies that describe the immigration process. According to them, this metaphor of uprooting is used to highlight the social stress involved in leaving one's native land as well as the difficulty of resettlement and adaptation in the new environment.

Ethnic group members who migrate from one culture to another face a number of changes in status. Several studies have shown (Banchevska, 1978; Fitinger & Schwartz, 1981; Sue & Morishima, 1982; Jones & Korchin, 1982) that immigration is usually stressful and often has serious psychological effects for several years after the event itself. This is especially true when there is no large well-established ethnic community into which the immigrant can be absorbed (Kiefer et al., 1985). For some, they are no longer the dominant group with intact values and traditions (New, Henderson, & Padgett, 1985). Some investigators have suggested that they face a "double jeopardy" of being elderly and ethnic in the new society. Another perspective suggests that aging is a "leveling experience" which virtually eliminates racial and ethnic inequalities of the younger years (New et al., 1985).

American and traditional Indian views of aging and the elderly are fairly divergent; it is likely that such differences may create conflicts and difficulties in the adaptation of elderly Asian Indians to America. Presented below is a review of the cultural ethos surrounding aging, and the aged in both cultures.

Values

Indian society is broadly influenced by norms, values, and traditions basic to the Hindu religion though the individualities of other religions are maintained and the religions influence one another (Desai & Khetani, 1979). Scriptural prescriptions within Hinduism emphasize filial piety as a recurrent theme. As featured in *Taittriya Upanisad*,

'*Maatru devo bhava, pitru devo bhava*' emphasize 'reverence of mother as God, reverence of father as God.'

Hindu seers examined the basic types of experience in men's lives that related to varying social systems such as family, society and religion, and thereby created the four stages of life to characterize such experiences. The four *ashramas* or stages: (a) *Brahmacharyashrama*, or the stage of a celibate learner, (b) *Grihastashrama*, or the stage of life as a householder, (c) *Vanaprasthashrama*, or the stage of gradual disengagement from worldly duties and loosening of social bonds. This involves a gradual withdrawal from family obligations, relegating householder duties to the background and bringing the ideal of renunciation to the foreground, and (d) *Sanyasashrama*, or the stage of complete disengagement leading to renunciation for achievement of spiritual freedom. There appears to be a parallel between this traditional Indian concept and the work of Cumming and Henry (1961) on disengagement theory (Vatuk, 1980). Their theory identified reduction of interaction with the environment among the elderly as being an eventual condition for the maintenance of life satisfaction.

On the other hand, American religious traditions are primarily from the Judeo-Christian heritage. In the United States, there is widespread commitment to the idea that activity is beneficial and maintenance of contact with the social environment is a condition for maintaining a sense of life satisfaction (Cowgill, 1986). This activity theory (Cavan, Burgess, Havighurst & Goldhammer, 1949) is based on achievement, work, and independence that are often considered prime American values. Havighurst (1972) posited in his theory of life-stage development that one of the developmental tasks of old age is, "Establishing an explicit affiliation with one's age group", thus stressing the importance of intragenerational contact.

Family

According to Ross (1970), in the Hindu system of family obligations, the sons are expected to look after their parents in old age and illness. If there are no sons, it is the duty of the daughters. After daughters, obligations fall on brothers, uncles, and finally, other relatives. There exists an element of obligation and collective responsibility for older members of the family. The traditional Indian social structure thus has a built-in arrangement for the care of the aged. But this traditional arrangement is undergoing slow but steady change.

Traditionally, the Hindu joint family is patriarchal in nature, the oldest male member is the head, holding the position of authority. Based on age, the elderly occupy positions of authority and respect, and their advice is sought in intrafamilial matters. The close family system in India provides a solid social support system for aged people, and the emphasis on spiritualism as opposed to materialism seems to help the elderly to lead a more peaceful and serene life (Sharma & Tiwari, 1983).

While the extended family in India vests considerable power and authority in the eldest male member, the situation is slightly different for older women. Although, she too is highly respected by the younger members of the family, her authority is somewhat restricted to female members of the family. Her primary responsibility is direction and distribution of work as well as ensuring assimilation of the family's traditional rules and regulations (Gore, 1978).

By contrast, the typical American family is predominantly nuclear and neolocal in form, and because children leave their parental residence at marriage and establish their homes elsewhere, parents are often left in an "empty nest" (Cowgill, 1986). Faucher (1979) discussed independence as an issue for older parents and their children with regard to living arrangements. Only widowhood or disability, not age per se, interrupts this pattern. Further, kinship ties are weakened by the mobility of the population as well as values of privacy and independence (Cowgill, 1986).

Though most older adults live in separate households, they are not necessarily socially isolated. Most of them have frequent and regular contacts with their children. It is estimated that 80% of all personal care and medically related services to older people in America continues to be provided by family members (Archbold, 1982).

In his book, "Growing old in America", Fischer (1979) argued that in early America elderly people were revered, respected and honored as a matter of general custom. He stated that 1607 to 1780 was a period of gerontophilia (love of old people). Between 1780 and 1820, however, there occurred a revolution in attitude toward the elderly that was characterized by gerontophobia (fear of old people). "This later revolution", he claimed, "heralded the emergence of a remarkable social phenomenon—the cult of youth. Hand in hand with the emergence of the cult of youth, there was a corresponding denigration of the elderly and a conspicuous loss of respect, care and concern."

Life Satisfaction

Successful aging and life satisfaction have been dominant themes in gerontological literature (Diener, 1984; Horley, 1984; Liang, 1985; Stock, Okun & Benin, 1986). Factors such as successful aging, adaptation to aging or positive adjustment to aging and old age have been identified as variables associated with feelings of subjective well-being or life satisfaction. Researchers regard life satisfaction as a useful construct and frequently use it as a criterion of successful aging (George & Bearon, 1980; Conte & Salamon, 1982; Salamon, 1988; Lawrence & Liang, 1988; Bearon, 1989).

In an Eastern culture like India, *nirmoha* (detachment), a prominent value of *Sanyasashrama* and *Vanaprasthashrama* (last two stages of Hindu life cycle), helps in accepting the inevitabilities of life, the impact of aging losses, and plays a role in life satisfaction (Motwani, 1986). *Sanyasashrama*, the last (fourth) stage of the Hindu life cycle, prescribes disengagement from material pursuits, freedom from family bonds, and self discipline to conquer five basic human drives—*kama* (sensual pleasure), *krodha* (anger), *lobha* (greed), *moha* (attachment), and *ahamkar* (egoism, vanity). It is recommended that older persons replace disengagement by active engagement in inner peace, ego integration, self-awareness, discipline and self-realization (Motwani, 1986).

By contrast, in Western culture, sense of happiness, sense of self-fulfillment, sense of self-worth, sense of self-contentment, acceptance of old age, acceptance of life's failure and success, positive self-image, and optimistic views toward life and others are collectively thought of as life satisfaction (Lawton, 1972; Neugarten, 1976).

FACTORS RELATED TO LIFE SATISFACTION

Life satisfaction, as related to the realities of the aging process implies that the individual is considered as "being at the positive end of the continuum of psychological well-being" (Neugarten, Havighurst & Tobin, 1961). Further, in that "life in general" or "life as a whole" is the referent, a long-range perspective is implied.

Numerous variables have been identified as related to life satisfaction and used to explain differences in life satisfaction within and between groupings of people. Sex differences in life satisfaction are a recurrent research topic in social gerontology (Liang, 1982). Studies of the relationship of sex to life satisfaction have been reported with mixed results (Quinn, 1980). While Liang (1982) determined no sex differences in life satisfaction, other studies have shown that men reported higher levels of satisfaction (Jackson, Chatters, & Neighbors, 1982; Sauer, 1977). Historically, men and women in India have enjoyed different statuses and played different roles. In light of the differing status, roles, and expectations for elderly Asian Indian men and women, investigating sex differences is important for this investigation.

Research by Maguire (1981) identified health, social support and educational level as significantly related to life satisfaction. The majority of studies show a slight decline in well being with age (Larson, 1978). Income, occupational status, and education have been related to well being (Larson, 1978). Leonard (1981) found marital status, occupational prestige, years of formal education, race, and annual income associated with successful aging. Several studies have highlighted the relationship between social interaction and life satisfaction (Kohen, 1983; Gottlieb, 1983; Ward, 1985). Limited access to transportation has been discussed as an important factor of adjustment for aged Asian Indians in the United States (Sikri, 1989).

Faucher (1979) emphasized living arrangements as important for older people and that different living arrangements can explain variance in reported life satisfaction. Han (1986) reported that the longer Korean elderly immigrants lived in the United States, the greater their social interaction with friends and voluntary organizations. Chan (1988) discussed the plight of elderly refugees as different from immigrants, making reasons for coming to the United States an important consideration.

Globally, life satisfaction is regarded as an individual's subjective view of the overall quality of life (Andrews and Withey, 1976). On the other hand, domain-specific measures are an additional approach that focus on specific aspects of life that have significance to most people and contribute to the overall quality of one's life (Campbell, Converse & Rodgers, 1976; Campbell, 1981). Campbell (1981) delineated twelve major domains of life: marriage, family life, friendship, standard of living/material goods, work, neighborhood, city/town of residence, nation, housing, education, health, and self.

This study examined life satisfaction, both globally and with regard to domain specific measures among elderly immigrant Asian Indians living in the United States. In other words, besides the larger picture of general well being of the individual, specific areas of concern or domain specific measures were addressed. Further, open-ended questions presented to respondents provided an opportunity to discuss cultural differences, feelings about life in the United States, and perceptions of one's status here.

Variables selected for this study

The literature suggests that the following variables are important, therefore they have been selected as significant in assessing the levels of life satisfaction for immigrant Asian Indian elderly in the United States. They include (a) *socio-demographic characteristics*: - sex, age, marital status, education, employment status, reasons for coming to the United States, length of stay in the United States, and (b) *domain variables*. Included as domain variables are - living arrangement (living relationships and type of housing), transportation (mode of transportation and access to transportation), self-assessed health (health rating and present health evaluation), finance, and social interaction number and average interactions with family and friends.

RESEARCH QUESTIONS

This study proposed to answer the following questions:

1. What are the levels of life satisfaction among immigrant Asian Indian elderly presently residing in the United States?

2. Are there sex differences in levels of life satisfaction among immigrant Asian Indian elderly presently residing in the United States?

3. What factors explain differences in levels of life satisfaction among older immigrant Asian Indian men and women presently residing in the United States?

a. Do the following socio-demographic characteristics (age, sex, marital status, education, employment, reasons for coming to the United States, length of stay in the United States) account for differences in levels of life satisfaction among immigrant Asian Indian elderly men and women presently residing in the United States?

b. Do the following domain variables (living arrangement, transportation, self-assessed health, finance, and social interaction) account for differences in levels of life satisfaction among immigrant Asian Indian elderly men and women presently residing in the United States?

DEFINITION OF TERMS

The following terms are defined as they are used in this study.

Life Satisfaction

The extent to which individuals take pleasure from the round of activities that constitute everyday life. Whether they regard life as meaningful and accept that which life has been, feel success in achieving major goals, hold a positive image of self, and maintain happy and optimistic attitudes and mood, they are regarded as satisfied with life (Neugarten, Havighurst, & Tobin, 1961). The instruments used to measure life satisfaction in this study, have a content that reflects the operational definition given by Neugarten, Havighurst, and Tobin (1961).

Finance

Examines the adequacy of one's financial situation relative to needs.

Self-assessed health

A self-perception of health that asks respondents to rate their health as one of the following: excellent, good, fair, poor, very poor. In addition, an evaluation of health relative to things one can or cannot do.

Transportation

State the typical mode of transportation used, and an assessment of the availability of transportation when needed.

Living arrangement

Looks at the type of housing that respondents live in, as well as identifies whom the individual lives with.

Social interaction

Considers the number, frequency of average meeting, and average talk/correspondence with both family and friends.

II
Review of Literature

The review of literature is divided into the following sections: (a) Life Satisfaction, (b) Aging theories and life satisfaction, (c) Variables associated with life satisfaction, and (d) Cultural background (Asian Indian elderly).

LIFE SATISFACTION

A major concern in the field of gerontology has been the measurement of psychological well being, long considered a strong indicator of "successful aging". Maddox and Campbell (1985) observed in the 'Handbook of Aging and the Social Sciences' that subjective well being was the most extensively investigated topic in social gerontology. To measure psychological well being, constructs such as life satisfaction, happiness, and morale have been put forth. They focus upon the assessment of inner states of older individuals; they assume that older persons themselves know best how they feel and can best assess their own psychological well being and happiness.

Life satisfaction and related constructs have enjoyed widespread appeal and use in social gerontology. George and Bearon (1980) stated, "If popularity is any indication of the usefulness of a concept, life satisfaction would be clearly indispensable, for gerontologists persistently use it as a criterion for successful aging."

George and Bearon (1980) reported the demonstrated relative stability of life satisfaction (Andrews & Withey, 1976) and its link to desired goals as making it a more attractive measure of subjective life quality to a research investigator than the more emotional and transitory reports of happiness. Further, they state that this is typically a more appealing concept than happiness to policy and social service professionals.

Despite its popular usage, there are several definitions of life satisfaction. Neugarten, Havighurst, and Tobin (1961) regarded individuals as satisfied to the extent that they take pleasure from the round of activities that constitute everyday life, regard life as meaningful and accept that which life has been, feel success in achieving major goals, hold a positive image of self, and maintain happy and optimistic attitudes and mood. Erikson (1959) defined life satisfaction in old age as the product of successfully resolving a series of psycho-social crises from infancy to old age. Stones and Kozma (1980) defined life satisfaction as "gratification of an appropriate portion of the major desires of life." Usui, Keil and Durig (1985) studied satisfaction with life as a function of the discrepancy between internalized standards and perceived realities.

Aging theories and life satisfaction

The following theories present varying viewpoints that are linked with life satisfaction. Two viewpoints—disengagement theory and activity theory have stimulated considerable research in this field. A third major theory, namely, continuity theory has begun to emerge in social gerontology in recent years. Erikson's theory of psychosocial development (1959) as related to successful aging is also discussed.

Cumming and Henry (1961) advanced the disengagement theory of aging as a functional approach to social interaction. This refers to a mutual withdrawal by the elderly from society and a withdrawal by society from the elderly. In other words, successful aging is related to the gradual withdrawal from social roles and positions, in preparation for death.

By contrast, activity theorists (Cavan, Burgess, Havighurst & Goldhammer, 1949) assert that successful aging reflects the individual's ability to maintain the performance of roles and activities that existed during earlier stages in the life cycle. This theory suggests that despite role loss or role change for the elderly person, one should not withdraw from social activity; instead, role loss should be successfully replaced with another, similar activity.

Howe (1987) reported that several authors in gerontology (Atchley, 1980; Crandall, 1980; Dowd, 1981) have discussed the literature that compares and contrasts, defines and delimits, supports and attacks these well-known social theories of aging. Their common conclusion is that for both substantive and methodological reasons, neither theory is regarded as adequate to fully explain the myriad patterns of adjustment to aging.

Since neither activity theory nor disengagement theory adequately accounts for individual differences in aging, many researchers are proposing that personality may be the key element influencing life satisfaction. Continuity theory proposed by Neugarten (1964) holds that one would expect individuals to continue those interactional behaviors or predispositions that served them well throughout life. In other words, if the individual were socially involved and active, activity may be expected to continue. On the other hand, if the individual were withdrawn, one could expect disengagement in later life. At every phase of the life cycle, these predispositions constantly evolve from interactions among personal preferences, biological and psychological capabilities, situational opportunities, and experience. Change is therefore considered an adaptive process that involves interaction among all of these elements.

Unlike the activity theory, continuity theory does not assume that lost roles need to be replaced. While disengagement and activity theory predict one single direction that an individual's adaptation to aging will take, continuity theory holds that adaptation can go in one of several directions. While such complexity may give continuity theory an edge in terms of explaining the full picture of aging, this same complexity has the disadvantage of being difficult to conceptualize, measure and analyze. Though this theory does not easily lend itself to experimental validation, it provides a general framework that explains how the disengagement theory and the activity theory, while being theoretically distinct, can both be useful explanations of older persons' ability to be satisfied with their lives. Continuity theory is one of the most complex in social gerontology, and is backed by much less research. Nevertheless, it is considered the most promising one.

The last perspective considered here is that of Erik Erikson (1959) who described human development in terms of eight psychosocial stages. According to him, an individual in the last stage looks upon his past to determine whether his life has been fulfilled. In doing so, he may accept life for what it is and thus acquire integrity and ego strength. However, if he feels dissatisfied, and has difficulty making changes, he feels despair. In other words, a successful ager has achieved what may be called integrity.

The usefulness of this theory rests largely in the insights that it provides from examining the lives of individuals within the context of the theory. Again, this theory also does not easily lend itself to experimental validation, but provides a general framework for describing some of the major changes that occur in the life span.

Variables associated with life satisfaction

For the ensuing section, a review of studies related to life satisfaction and variables under consideration in this study are described. The independent variables in this study are (a) socio-demographic characteristics, including sex, age, marital status, employment status, reasons for coming to the United States, length of stay in the United States, and education, and (b) domain variables, including living arrangement, transportation, self-assessed health, finance, and social interaction.

Sex

Despite numerous studies, the empirical evidence concerning sex differences in life satisfaction is by no means conclusive (Liang, 1982). While some studies have confirmed sex differences (Negron, 1987; Shebani, 1984; Suh, 1987; Eu, 1987), others have found no evidence for such differences (Lawrence and Liang, 1988; Rhodes, 1980; Collette, 1984; Chou, 1987). When looking at the relationship between selected variables and life satisfaction for older men and women, sex differences have been demonstrated as minimal and are often inconsistent.

Studying sex differences among Asian Indian elderly is a crucial examination, as Indian men and women have historically enjoyed different statuses. Status, authority and property were possessions of the male descent group, and typically inheritance was passed from father to son (Kapadia, 1986). The situation however, was radically different for women of the post-Vedic age (Rao & Rao, 1981). Until educational reforms evolved in the eighteenth century, denial of education, subordination and subservience in all stages of life—in childhood to father, in youth to husband and elderly kin, and to sons when widowed, was prescribed (Rao & Rao, 1981).

Early twentieth century women in India continued to occupy an inferior position within the family; her only hope for increased status was in the birth of sons and onset of old age. Even in old age, older women were obliged to respect the authority of male members. However, with increasing age there was some loosening of such obligations.

Age

As Larson (1978) reported, advancing age is related to a decline in subjective well being among people over age sixty. However, numerous studies have shown this decline to be a product of other negative factors that influence the well being of the very old. Other factors may include loss of health, fewer financial resources, widowhood, and loss of friends (Edwards & Klemmack. 1973; Kivett, 1976; Larson, 1975).

Marital Status

Using Life Satisfaction Index-A, Strumpf (1982) found no evidence for marital status influencing life satisfaction in a study of older women in the city of New York. However, several researchers have reported a positive relationship between marital status and life satisfaction (Knapp, 1976; Medley, 1980; Leonard, 1981). While Reinhardt (1988) found married respondents showed higher life satisfaction than widowed respondents, Kohen (1983) reported marital status as an ongoing force in life satisfaction. Overall, there appears to be a slight independent relation between marital status and subjective well being.

Employment

Thompson (1973) described a positive association between employment and well being among older people. Using Life Satisfaction Index-Z, Negron (1987) found life satisfaction to be moderately high among retirees. However, since the decision to retire is interlinked with factors such as health, it is not possible to conclusively infer that this relationship is attributable to retirement alone. At present, we can conclude that the relationship between employment and life satisfaction is unclear.

Education

Several studies show a small correlation between education and life satisfaction, especially when statistical controls are introduced (Edwards & Klemmack, 1973; Markides & Martin, 1979). Using Life Satisfaction Index-Z, Maguire (1981) found education to be significantly related to life satisfaction. Leonard (1981) assessed the empirical relationship between life satisfaction and twenty-three socio/demographic/psychological factors. Data analysis indicated that education was one of the variables related to successful aging. However, Usui, Keil and Durig (1985) found education does not have a direct effect on life satisfaction.

Finance

Income was one of the variables that was found to be a strong predictor of life satisfaction (Spreitzer & Snyder, 1974; Mancini, Quinn, Gavigan & Franklin, 1980; Medley, 1980; Berghorn & Schaefer, 1981; Leonard, 1981; Walsh, 1986). Fletcher and Lorenz (1985) investigated the relationship between objective and subjective indicators of economic well being within different age, race, and gender groups. They found relationships to remain stable within all subgroups over time. Using Life Satisfaction Index-A, Suh (1987) found some of the variance in life satisfaction of older Americans to be explained by self-perceived financial status.

Liang and Fairchild (1979) put forth the concept of 'relative deprivation' in explaining the relationship between income and perceived financial adequacy. For example, if an older person has a relatively low income but believes he is better off than his reference others, he is likely to be satisfied. Conversely, an aged person with a higher income may be dissatisfied because he feels he is worse off than others (Liang, Dvorkin, Kahana & Mazian, 1980).

Access to transportation

Skolgund (1986) emphasized the importance of transportation for the elderly, as shopping for food, obtaining health services, social support and interaction are heavily dependent on it. Similarly, Han (1986) pointed out that adequate transportation tremendously benefits older persons by facilitating their integration into society as well as their use of its resources.

In Han's (1986) study, nearly fifty percent of immigrant Korean elders reported that the lack of transportation was one of the most difficult problems that they had to face in America. Lack of transportation was a major problem reported by Chan (1988) who cited the expression "no legs" as commonly used by Asian elderly in the United States who complain of severe handicaps due to transportation.

Living arrangement

Living accommodation and living with children were salient variables in explaining life satisfaction of older Asian Americans (Suh, 1987). Toledo (1982) concluded that housing was one of two most important factors explaining perceived life satisfaction among elderly females. According to Han (1986), the place where elderly individuals reside could be one of several factors that affect social participation and well being. Similarly, Faucher (1979) identified housing as an important variable in explaining variance in life satisfaction.

Data on Asian Indian elderly suggest that having more kin in the United States reduces the likelihood of living alone (Burr, 1992). Using 1990 Census public use microdata sample, Himes (1996) reported that institutional living is rare among Asians compared to African Americans and white Americans.

Reasons for coming to the United States

According to Chan (1988), the situation is radically different for elderly refugees than immigrants living with children. Unlike most other immigrants, elderly refugees could not reasonably expect to be able to return to their countries of origin if life here proved too difficult. Therefore, it seems that the circumstances or reasons for coming to the United States may be an important consideration in examining life satisfaction of Asian Indian elderly immigrants.

Length of stay

Length of residence is an important variable, particularly for immigrants settled in a foreign land, where this could be a distinctive indicator for the levels of acculturation and assimilation.

Koh, Sakauye, Koh and Liu (1984), found that length of residence correlated significantly with English vocabulary, cohabitation, social support and economic resources among Korean elderly in the Chicago area. It has been reported by Hurh & Kim (1984), Hurh, Kim and Kim (1978), that in the early exigency period (1-2 years after immigration), language barriers, unemployment or underemployment, and social isolation reach their peak. Han (1986) identified length of residence in America as a significant variable affecting life satisfaction among 192 Koreans living in the Chicago Metropolitan area.

Social interaction

Several studies have highlighted the importance of interpersonal relations to life satisfaction in gerontological literature (Ward, 1985; Liang et al., 1980; Snow & Crapo, 1982; Cicirelli, 1981; Gottlieb, 1983; Stoller & Earl, 1983; Kohen, 1983).

Han (1986) found interaction with family members to be the most important factor affecting the general well being of older Koreans settled in America. While Burgio (1987) described contact with friends as being positively related to life satisfaction, Skolgund (1986) found contact with friends as more important to life satisfaction than contact with family.

Self-assessed health

Advancing age brings with it potential illnesses, infirmities, and declining faculties that can hamper an individual's life style and limit his or her overall satisfaction with life.

Several researchers have identified health status as a strong indicator of life satisfaction and well being (Toseland & Rasch, 1979; George & Landerman, 1984; Mancini et al., 1980). Using a mail survey of 1,650 respondents, Wiliest and Crider (1988) found health ratings to be significantly correlated with overall life satisfaction, community satisfaction, job satisfaction, and marital satisfaction. Other researchers have shown this relationship as significant even when other variables are introduced (Markides & Martin, 1979; Graney & Zimmerman, 1980).

George and Landerman (1984) reported subjective evaluations of health as being consistently and positively related to well-being ratings among older as well as general populations. Cockerham (1983) identified the perception of one's health status as an important indicator of the manner in which aged persons related to their social world. Typically, the healthier the individual perceives oneself to be the greater the life satisfaction reported.

Health was isolated as an important determinant of life satisfaction and self-report was identified as a valid indicator of health among older adults by Weinberger et al., (1986). Ferraro (1980) reported evidence from a national survey of 3,402 older persons that indicated that self-ratings of health are significantly related to measures of objective health status and thus are an economical means of gaining information about the health of the elderly.

Research by the American Association of Retired Persons (AARP) suggests that Asian elderly do not make use of health services as readily as their white counterparts in the United States. They are likely to hold off on the use of long-term care needs. Many older Asians indicated a preference for traditional medicines and practitioners, and reported language barriers as a major deterrent to use of formal health services.

CULTURAL BACKGROUND

The experience of aging differs in different cultures and subcultural groups, thus displaying tremendous cultural diversity. As alluded to earlier, the American and traditional Indian views of aging and the elderly are fairly divergent, and this may create problems and difficulties for immigrant Asian Indian elderly living in the United States. Asian Indian elderly immigrants to America are products of a culture with a more favorable view of aging. A few Hindu religion doctrines as well as cultural values related to aging, and the joint family system are discussed to provide an in-depth understanding.

Hindu perspectives

As explained by Motwani (1986), Hindus believe that unlike the body, the soul is immortal. After death, one is born again and therefore subject to the cycle of births and deaths. Birth and death are considered as two stages of life, analogous to sunrise and sunset.

In Tilak's (1989) book, 'Religion and Aging in the Indian tradition', the foreword written by Katherine Young offers some insights into the Hindu stages of life or 'ashramas'. According to Young (1989), Hindu thinkers examined the basic types of experience in men's lives that related to varying social systems such as family, society and religion, and thereby created the four stages of life to characterize such experiences.

Each of the four stages or *ashramas* has a distinct order or purpose. The first stage is that of *Brahmacharyashrama* or studentship, where the seeds of worldly life are sown, the individual is educated for a future occupation and the skills needed to accomplish the next stage of life. There is considerable training in chastity, concentration, and discipline. The second stage is of *Grihastashrama* or married life where the individual is fully engaged in his occupation and familial duties (including the duty to have children). This stage also encourages individuals to set aside time for prayers, pilgrimages, and yogic exercises. The third stage of Hindu life is *Vanaprasthashrama* and this involves a gradual withdrawal from family obligations, relegating householder duties to the background and bringing the ideal of renunciation to the foreground. The final stage of complete renunciation (*Sanyasashrama*) provides the freedom and calm to contemplate the experiences of life.

Erik Erikson (1969) defined *Vanaprasthashrama* as the inner separation from all ties of self-hood, body bondedness; communality and their replacement by a striving which will eventually lead to 'Moksha', renunciation, and disappearance. The achievement of the third stage of life lay in the discipline and gradual renunciation of familial ties and social relations. Although one's affiliations and associations with various community groups have come to an end, one's obligations and duties to society persisted (Kapadia, 1986).

The duties of the last stage were mainly defined with attaining detachment. In other words, society was overshadowed by a man's concern with his own realization of spirituality. But this did not mean his social obligations completely ceased (Kapadia, 1986). In present day situations, the values of *Sanyasashrama* that include *nirmoha* (detachment) and self-realization are generally practiced within the family context, living with children and grandchildren. It is not uncommon for many elderly Indians to withdraw from their homes, and travel to sacred places. Their extended pilgrimage over long periods of time is akin to the wandering ascetic (Young, 1989).

Vatuk (1980) while describing the parallel between disengagement theory and the Hindu stages of life, points out that the Hindu formulation is more unidimensional. "It prescribes a code for action by the individual, for his own spiritual well-being. It is a normative concept which says nothing about psychological, developmental reality." Nonetheless, the existence of such a concept among Hindus in

India is of tremendous relevance in assessing disengagement theory in a cross-cultural perspective.

Family

An understanding of the traditional Indian family is important; however, in the face of modernization, the family as an institution is changing. In traditional Indian society, old age is considered a "storehouse" of knowledge and wisdom. The aged are generally looked upon with respect and reverence (Desai & Khetani, 1979). The joint family system provides security through mutuality of relationships and encourages interdependence. Children assume responsibility for the care of their parents as part of *dharma* or duty.

In modern India, a phenomenal increase in the number of aged people is already creating problems of an unprecedented nature. The widespread prevalence of the joint family in India was for generations a guarantee for the care and protection for the aged. However, the social landscape of India is rapidly changing. The role and status of the older adult is intertwined with the values, economics and politics of the society they live in. Against the backdrop of growing modernization, rising dual-career families, and disintegration of the joint family, policy makers are challenged with providing a framework for care of the elderly.

Using Life Satisfaction Index-A (LSI-A), Cantril Self-anchoring ladder, and a semi-structured interview, Thomas and Chambers (1989) compared the responses of fifty elderly Indian men from New Delhi, India and a sample of British male respondents from London, England. While no significant differences were reported on the structured measures, there was considerable difference in the responses of the two groups based on a qualitative analysis. Elderly Indians residing in India reported family closeness as being primarily linked to life satisfaction. On the other hand, the dominant theme for the British sample was fear of incapacitation, of becoming dependent and useless.

Status

Those Asian Indians coming from a culture where elderly held respected statuses now find themselves growing old in a culture where older people are not regarded in the same manner. Given that a sizeable portion of their lives has been spent in the Indian societal context where socio-cultural conditions are remarkably different, the situation calls for considerable adjustment. Being uprooted is stressful, as such dislocation results in tremendous difficulty with communication, loss of sensory contact with a familiar environment, as well the learning of new behavior patterns (Coelho, Ahmed & Yuan, 1980).

When Asian elders come to the United States, their role and status are often reversed. They may no longer be served and consulted as head of the family; instead, they are often powerless and dependent on adult children to help manage their lives. "Under house arrest" is how several elderly Asian Indian immigrants described their existence to Sikri (1989) in an interview reported in the newspaper, 'India Abroad'. As Sikri (1989) reported, "Living with their children in suburban neighborhoods, with minimal public transportation, unable to drive, in several instances, unable to communicate because of language barriers, many aged Indian immigrants are relegated to the job of 'babysitters' for their grandchildren". The other half of those interviewed by Sikri (1989), expressed "a sense of tremendous satisfaction at a serene and meaningful life with their families and grandchildren."

III
Methods

The objective of this research was to explore the level of life satisfaction among immigrant Asian Indian elderly, and to examine the influence of selected variables on the level of life satisfaction.

This chapter presents (a) Characteristics of participants, (b) Research instruments, (c) Procedure used in data collection, and (d) Data analysis.

CHARACTERISTICS OF PARTICIPANTS

In this study, the criteria for subject selection included being (a) born outside the United States, (b) permanently settled in the United States since age fifty, or later (c) presently aged sixty or above, (d) permanent resident of the United States for two or more years, and (e) English speaking adult.

An overview describing the participants in this study was obtained from the devised Interview Schedule (see Appendix A). This schedule asked participants to describe themselves on the socio-demographic variables of age, sex, marital status, employment, reasons for coming to the United States, and length of stay in the United States. In addition to socio-demographic variables, information was sought regarding the following domain variables of living arrangement (living relationships and type of housing), transportation (mode of transportation and access to transportation), self-assessed health (health rating and present health evaluation), finance, and social interaction (number and average interactions with family and friends).

Socio-demographics

Subjects in this study consisted of fifty Asian Indian immigrant elderly men and women residing in the Washington, D.C. metropolitan area. Twenty-five men and twenty-five women participated in this study.

Though respondents were of varying religious backgrounds, they were predominantly Hindus (82%). The remaining respondents were Sikhs (10%), Jains (4%), Moslems (2%), and Buddhists (2%). Of those who reported being Sikhs, the majority of them were women. No other sex difference with religious affiliation was observed.

Age

The age of the respondents ranged from 60-90 years with 68.70 emerging as the average age (SD = 6.20). Approximately, half (54%) of those interviewed were between the ages of 60 and 69. While greater percentage of women were in the age group of 60-64, a greater number of men reported being in the age group of 70-74 (see Table 1).

Table 1
Frequency and percentage of the age of respondents

Variables	Women (N=25)		Men (N=25)		Total	
	Freq.	%	Freq.	%	Freq.	%
Age						
60-64	11	22	07	14	18	36
65-69	05	10	04	08	09	18
70-74	06	12	10	20	16	32
75-79	01	2	02	4	03	6
80-84	01	2	02	4	03	6
85-90	01	2	00	0	01	2

Marital status

The original five categories of marital status were reduced to two categories of married and not married. The group of non-married respondents included those who were single, widowed, separated or divorced. Sixty-four percent of the respondents were married, and thirty-six percent were not married. About eight percent of the respondents interviewed were husband and wife from the same household. Older women were twice as likely to report being not married as were older men (see Table 2).

Table 2
Frequency and percentage of marital status

Variables	Women (N=25)		Men (N=25)		Total	
	Freq.	%	Freq.	%	Freq.	%
Marital Status						
Not married	12	24	06	12	18	36
Married	13	26	19	38	32	64

Education

Educational attainment varied among those interviewed. Again, this category was reduced to two, with approximately half (52%) having less than a college degree and the rest (48%) having a college or more advanced degree. A sex difference in the level of education was observed. While more than half the older women reported having less than a college degree, more than half the older men interviewed indicated that they had a college or more advanced degree (Table 3).

Employment

Most of the respondents were not employed (74%). Of those not employed, forty-two percent were women and about thirty-two percent were men. Those who remained in the work force primarily maintained such jobs as Babysitters, Accountants, Teachers, and Real Estate

Brokers. Of those who reported employment, older men were twice more likely to work than older women. Average hours for those employed was 10.86 per week, the range was 4-55 (see Table 3).

Table 3
Frequency and percentage of education and employment

Variables	Women (N=25)		Men (N=25)		Total	
	Freq.	%	Freq.	%	Freq.	%
Education						
No college degree	16	32	10	20	26	52
college degree	09	18	15	30	24	48
Employment						
Not working	21	42	16	32	37	74
Working	04	8	09	18	13	26

Reasons for coming to the United States

The majority of the aged respondents in this study reported that they came to the United States to be with family. While majority (75%) of the older female respondents indicated that they came to the United States to be with family, only sixty percent of older male respondents gave the same reason.

Nearly sixty-eight percent of this sample recounted that they were somewhat or very happy when they made the decision to leave India and settle permanently in the United States. Older men and women did not differ on the degree of happiness they experienced when they made this decision.

About one-fourth of those interviewed said they alone made the decision to come to the United States. Three times as many men indicated that they alone made the decision than older women participants. However, a higher percentage (34%) reported that their children made the decision for them. No sex differences were observed among respondents whose children made the decision that they settle in the United States (see Table 4).

Table 4

Frequency and percentage of reasons for coming to the United States and length of stay in the United States

Variables	Women (N=25)		Men (N=25)		Total	
	Freq.	%	Freq.	%	Freq.	%
Reasons for coming to the US						
Economic	00	0	03	6	03	6
Family	21	42	14	28	35	70
Other	04	8	08	16	12	24
Length of stay						
2-5 years	08	16	08	16	16	32
6-9 years	10	20	08	16	18	36
10-14 years	05	10	06	12	11	22
15-19 years	01	2	01	2	02	4
20-30 years	01	2	02	4	03	6

Length of stay in the United States

About sixty-eight percent of the respondents had been in the United States for less than ten years. For those interviewed, the average length of stay in the United States was 8.20 years, the range was 2-26 years (SD=8.20). The majority of this sample (84%) had never lived for six months or longer in any other country besides India and the United States.

Since their permanent residence in the United States, the majority (84%) of those interviewed indicated that they had visited India. Those who visited India were more likely to do so once every two to three years. One-third of those who had visited India reported that their stay in India was typically a month long. No sex differences were observed among respondents with frequency of visits to India as well as length of stay in India (see Table 4).

Domain Variables

Living arrangement

In describing their living arrangement, majority of those interviewed (72%) indicated that they were living with their children, followed by those who reported that they were living with their spouse (22%). Most respondents reported living in their children's home (56%), and about twenty-two percent indicated that they lived in their own home or apartment (see Table 5). Further, it was observed that respondents were as likely to live with their female offspring as their male children.

All respondents were asked, "If you had a choice would you choose an alternate arrangement?" In this study, an overwhelming majority (92%) of men and women responded, "No".

Table 5

Frequency and percentage of living arrangement

Variables	Women (N=25)		Men (N=25)		Total	
	Freq.	%	Freq.	%	Freq.	%
Living arrangement						
Type of housing						
Own house/apt.	05	10	06	12	11	22
Rented house/apt.	01	2	01	2	02	4
Children's home	15	30	13	26	28	56
Children's apt.	02	4	02	4	04	8
Apt. for elderly	01	2	02	4	03	6
Relative's home	01	2	00	0	01	2
Non-rel's. home	00	0	01	2	01	2
Living relationships						
Live alone	00	0	02	4	02	4
Live w/spouse	05	10	06	12	11	22
Live w/ children	19	38	17	34	36	72
Live w/relatives	01	2	00	0	01	2

Most respondents indicated that they were active participants in activities involving themselves and their own households. The majority of respondents reported cooking or preparing meals on a daily basis (64%), doing own laundry (62%), and running personal errands (38%). About forty-two percent of this sample reported doing yard work.

This sample also expressed active participation in activities involving others'. Of those fifty interviewed, babysitting grandchildren was reported by approximately half (42%) the respondents, and babysitting other children was reported by five respondents (10%). More than half of those interviewed reported babysitting other children on a daily basis. Only three of a total of fifty participants interviewed (6%) mentioned that they provided rides to others.

Older men and women differed on participation in various household activities. For instance, women were twice as likely to baby-sit their grandchildren as well as other children than older men were. Similarly, older women were most likely to cook or help prepare meals. However, older men were twice as likely to provide rides to others and run errands than older women were. No sex differences were observed for other household activities.

Self-assessed health

The health ratings indicated by a majority of this sample (74%) ranged from good to excellent. The average rating on health was 3.88 (SD= .91), representing good to excellent health. The number of older men and women who rated their health as excellent varied. While older women were less likely to rate their health as excellent (4%), older men were much more likely to give this rating (20%).

An evaluation of present health relative to things that an individual can or cannot do was sought. Men were more likely than women to evaluate their present state of health as enabling them to do nearly all of the things they wanted to do. On the other hand, women were more likely to evaluate their present state of health as a limiting factor with some of the things they wanted to do (see Table 6).

Table 6

Frequency and percentage of self-assessed health

Variables	Women (N=25)		Men (N=25)		Total	
	Freq.	%	Freq.	%	Freq.	%
Self-assessed health						
Present health (allows me to)						
do some of things	11	22	03	6	14	28
do most of things	08	16	11	22	19	38
do all of things	06	12	11	22	17	34
Health rating						
Very poor	00	0	01	2	01	2
Poor	03	6	00	0	03	6
Fair	08	16	01	2	09	18
Good	12	24	13	26	25	50
Excellent	02	4	10	20	12	24

Finance

A subjective report of the financial situation of all participants' was sought relative to their needs. With regard to financial satisfaction, the average score obtained was 2.30 (SD= .61) representing a financial situation that is adequate relative to one's needs.

Approximately half of those interviewed reported their financial situation as adequate for their needs. Only eight percent of this sample described their finances as less than adequate for their needs (Table 7).

Table 7
Frequency and percentage of finance

Variables	Women (N=25)		Men (N=25)		Total	
	Freq.	%	Freq.	%	Freq.	%
Finance						
Less than adeq.	01	2	03	6	04	8
Adequate	14	28	13	26	27	54
More than adeq.	10	20	09	18	19	38

Transportation

With regard to transportation, respondents were asked to identify the most typical mode of transportation as well as comment on access to transportation. While riding with others was most frequently cited as a means of getting around (54%), about one-fourth of those interviewed (24%) reported using public transportation.

Majority of respondents described that they often or always had access to transportation (92%). The mean score obtained was 3.42 (SD= .70). In this study, older men nearly twice more often reported total access to transportation than women (see Table 8).

Table 8

Frequency and percentage of transportation

Variables	Women (N=25)		Men (N=25)		Total	
	Freq.	%	Freq.	%	Freq.	%
Transportation						
Mode of transportation						
Walk	00	0	01	2	01	2
By own car	00	0	09	18	09	18
Borrow car	00	0	01	2	01	2
Public transp.	03	6	09	18	12	24
Ride with others	22	44	05	10	27	54
Access to transportation						
Rarely or Never	00	0	01	2	01	2
Sometimes	02	4	01	2	03	6
Often	14	28	06	12	20	40
Always	09	18	17	34	26	52

Social interaction (family)

All respondents (100%) replied affirmatively when asked if they had family members residing in the United States. As mentioned earlier, the average number of family members that respondents reported in the United States was eight. Of those fifty participants interviewed, men were more likely (24%) to have eight or more family members in the United States than women (14%).

Nearly eighty percent of this sample reported that they had between one to four children living in the United States. While a few respondents (16%) reported that they had no grandchildren in the United States, the rest indicated that they had between one to nine grandchildren. While none of the fifty respondents had a parent, uncle or aunt in the United States, the majority of respondents indicated that they had no siblings (70%), no cousins (86%), and no nephews or nieces (70%) in the United States.

Of those interviewed, thirty-four percent described the average frequency of meeting their children as everyday, while a higher percent (40%) confirmed meeting them on a weekly basis. Similarly, forty percent of the older respondents estimated meeting their grandchildren once a week. Those who had siblings in the United States pointed out that they saw their siblings three to four times a year. Those who had cousins as well as nephews and nieces living in the United States reported meeting them less than once a year.

On an average, the respondents in this study were more likely to maintain contact with family members through letters or by using the telephone. Older respondents were more likely to talk/correspond with children (86%) and grandchildren (54%) on a daily basis, maintain contact on a weekly basis with siblings (8%), communicate with cousins on a monthly basis (6%), and keep in touch with nephews and nieces, once in three to four months (14%).

Table 9

Frequency and percentage of social interaction (family)

Variables	Women (N=25)		Men (N=25)		Total	
	Freq.	%	Freq.	%	Freq.	%
Social Interaction (family)						
Number of family members						
Less than av.	14	28	11	22	25	50
Average	04	8	02	4	06	12
More than av.	07	14	12	24	19	38
Average meeting family members						
Less than av.	07	14	08	16	15	30
Average	06	12	13	26	19	38
More than av.	12	24	04	8	16	32
Average talk/correspond family						
Less than av.	06	12	09	18	15	30
Average	09	18	07	14	16	32
More than av.	10	20	09	18	19	38

Average frequency of meeting every listed family member was recorded using the scale 0-5 (see Interview schedule in Appendix A). Since there are seven listed family members, the potential range of scores that could be obtained was 0-35. This score represented overall average meetings with family.

In this study, respondents obtained a range of 1-16 with 8.3 as the mean score. This average score indicates limited number of meetings with family members by this sample. About 70% of the participants scored 8.3 or above. In this study, on an average, women were more likely to report higher number of meetings with family members than men.

A similar computation was carried out for average talk/correspondence with family members, so that a score range of 0-35 could be generated. However, the obtained range was 2-18, including a higher average score of 10.48. Again, this average score indicates limited talk/correspondence with family members by those participants that were interviewed. Similar to the finding on average frequency of meeting family members, about 70% of the respondents scored at or above the average score for average talk/correspondence with family members (see Table 9).

Social interaction (friends)

The average number of friends in the United States was reported to be approximately five to nine. Of those fifty older men and women that were interviewed, nearly half (46%) reported having ten or more friends, thirty-four percent reported having one to four friends, ten percent reported having five to nine friends, and ten percent said they had no friends in the United States. Those who reported that they had no friends in the United States were all older women.

Table 10

Frequency and percentage of social interaction (friends)

Variables	Women (N=25)		Men (N=25)		Total	
	Freq.	%	Freq.	%	Freq.	%
Number of friends in USA						
None	05	10	00	0	05	10
One to four	07	14	10	20	17	34
Five to nine	03	6	02	4	05	10
Ten or more	10	20	13	26	23	46
Average meeting friends						
No friends (NA)	05	10	00	0	05	10
Less than yearly	00	0	01	2	01	2
Few times a year	03	6	02	4	05	10
Monthly/bi-weekly	09	18	12	24	21	42
Weekly	08	16	09	18	17	34
Everyday	00	0	01	2	01	2
Average talk/correspond friends						
No friends (NA)	05	10	0	00	05	10
Few times a year	01	2	01	2	02	4
Monthly/bi-weekly	06	12	14	28	20	40
Weekly	12	24	07	14	19	38
Everyday	01	2	03	6	04	8

Average meetings with friends as well as average talk/correspondence with them was calculated. Of those interviewed, on an average, more than seventy-five percent reported meeting friends on a weekly to monthly basis. Only two percent of the sample interviewed reported meeting friends less than once a year.

The majority (74%) of participants indicated that the average talk/correspondence with friends was on a daily to monthly basis. None of the respondents reported talking/corresponding with friends less than once a year (see Table 10).

Lifestyle in India

In addition to the above, several questions regarding the life-style of participants when they lived in India was put forth. This was done to get an adequate picture of the background of all participants in this study.

A majority of those interviewed (70%) indicated that in India they lived in areas that they assessed as urban. Further, more than half (60%) of those interviewed indicated that they lived with their children. Nearly half (54%) of the respondents indicated that they were employed in India, and this group that reported employment was largely comprised of men. The most frequent jobs held in India were those of mid-level administrator, accountant, scientist, and small business owner. All respondents were asked to describe their financial situation in India. Nearly all respondents (94%) reported that their finances were adequate, or more than adequate relative to their needs.

The next question was about rating one's health when living in India. The five ratings employed in this study ranged from very poor to excellent. The majority of respondents interviewed rated their health in India as good or excellent (88%).

When living in India, public transportation was reported by fifty-two percent this sample as the most popular means of getting around. Further, the majority (86%) of those interviewed recalled that they had constant access to transportation whenever they needed it.

All respondents had family members when living in India. Of the fifty participants interviewed, it appeared that nearly all of them had a large social network of family and friends in India. The reported number of siblings, uncles/aunts, cousins, nephews and nieces in India, were approximately twice the number of those reported as living in the United States.

The majority of respondents (88%) indicated that they had five or more friends in India. They recalled meeting their friends on a daily/weekly basis (84%), and talking or corresponding with them on the same basis (88%).

RESEARCH INSTRUMENTS

The instruments used for data collection are described below. They were presented to respondents of this study in the following order: (a) Four open-ended questions, followed by the devised interview schedule that tapped background information as well as items that operationalized the independent variables in this study, (b) Life Satisfaction Index-B (LSI-B), & (c) Life Satisfaction Index-A (LSI-A).

Interview Schedule

The first question posed to respondents was a broad, global type question, "Tell me about life in America". The next two questions put forth the idea of "relative appreciation" (Atchley, 1982) or the feeling that one's condition is favorable in comparison to that of others' their age. Comparisons were sought between self and older persons in India as well as between self and older Americans. Finally, global, general well-being was assessed by this single item, "Taking everything into consideration, how would you describe your satisfaction with life?"

The Interview schedule devised by the researcher was used to gather background information about the subjects' age, sex, marital status, education, employment status, reasons for coming to the United States, and length of stay in the United States. Supplementary questions about previous life style in India were included to provide a description of the background of respondents in this study.

Besides information on socio-demographics, the Interview Schedule was also used to collect information on the following domain variables:

(a) *Transportation*: Included an assessment of typically used modes of transportation as well as a rating on access to transportation,

(b) *Living arrangement*: This examined type of housing as well as the nature of current living arrangement (alone or with others),

(c) *Finance*: This variable looked at self-perceived financial satisfaction relative to one's needs,

(d) *Social interaction*: Besides number of family members and friends, social interaction took into account average meeting times as well as average talk or correspondence made with family members and friends, and

(e) *Self-assessed health*: Self-perceived health rating as well as assessment of present state of health relative to what one would like to do.

Measures of Life Satisfaction

Neugarten, Havighurst, and Tobin (1961) developed the scale, Life Satisfaction Ratings (LSR) during the Kansas City Studies of Adult Life. Life Satisfaction Index -A (LSI-A) and Life Satisfaction Index- B (LSI-B) were devised from the basic LSR, which was used as the validating criterion (Neugarten et al., 1961). The two indices were to be used separately or together in studies where it is not possible to obtain the extensive data required to make LSR ratings.

Life Satisfaction Index has been reported as by far the most commonly used measure of life satisfaction among the elderly and one of the most carefully evaluated with regard to psychometric properties (George, 1981). This eighteen-item index with four components, is believed to represent the "complexity of psychological well-being" in older adults. Each item asks for agreement, disagreement or undecided as response options, and a total score is derived which represents the degree of satisfaction. Scores may range from 0 to 18, with higher scores representing higher levels of life satisfaction.

As mentioned earlier, the components of life satisfaction addressed by this measure are (a) mood tone, (b) zest versus apathy, (c) congruence between desired and achieved goals, and (d) resolution and fortitude. See Appendix A for a description of the items under each subscale of LSI-A.

Mood tone assesses the extent to which the respondent's life view is characterized by optimism and positive feelings. Those who score high on this dimension are happy with their lives and take pleasure in what they do. *Zest versus apathy* evaluates whether a respondent maintains a present and future life orientation, and whether that reflects hope and enthusiasm as opposed to resignation, listlessness and apathy.

Those individuals who score high on *congruence* reflect a sense of satisfaction as well as positive acceptance of their past. There has been a good fit between desires and accomplishments, and life has largely been what they wanted it to be. Neugarten (1967) has defined *resolution and fortitude* as the extent to which an individual accepts personal responsibility for his life and accepts in a relatively positive manner "that which life has been for him."

Life Satisfaction Index -B (LSI-B) is an open-ended questionnaire with a set scoring key for tallying life satisfaction points. LSI-B consists of twelve items (seven open-ended and five-checklist type) with 2 to 3 response categories. Scores may range from 0 to 23, with higher scores representing greater levels of life satisfaction.

As discussed in previous chapters, values of Indian culture differ substantially from Western ideas of life satisfaction. However, aging is a universal process (Kastenbaum, 1977) and considered inevitable, irrevocable, and an entity that affects everyone (Neugarten, 1976). A review of items in both instruments, LSI-A and LSI-B, clarify their applicability and potential usage in this study. For example, statements such as, "I feel old and somewhat tired", "As I look back on my life I am fairly well-satisfied", "I've gotten pretty much what I expected out of life" clearly have universal applications. Similarly, the same argument applies to LSI-B that includes questions such as, "What is the most important thing in your life right now?" and "How satisfied would you say you are with your way of life?".

Further, both measures focus upon the individual's internal frame of reference, rather than activity or social involvement. As Adams (1969) reported, LSI-A is claimed to be based on neither the activity nor the disengagement theory. Variables to be measured are the individuals own evaluation of his well being, thus minimizing any value judgements made by the investigator. As the authors of LSI-A and LSI-B stated, the assumption of the scale is that the "individual is the only proper judge of his well-being."

Reliability & Validity

Wolk and Kurtz (1975) reported a reliability coefficient of .84 (internal consistency) for Life Satisfaction Index -A. Rao and Rao (1981) found LSI-A as highly reliable on the basis of Discrimination (D-value) values for all items in the scale. Fawcett, Stonner, and Zepelin (1980) identified a retest reliability of .82 for the LSI-A when it was administered to a sample of elderly women four weeks after the initial testing.

Neugarten et al. (1961) found a correlation of .55 for the LSI-A and the original Life Satisfaction Index, and a correlation of .58 for the LSI-B. This suggests some degree of construct validity. The LSI-B was found to correlate .71 with the Life Satisfaction Ratings (LSR) and .73 with the LSI-A (Havighurst, 1963).

In investigating construct validity of various scales of psychological well being, Lohmann (1977) computed Pearson Product Moment correlation coefficients for frequently used measures of life satisfaction. The intercorrelations between LSI-A and other scales were as follows: Cavan Adjustment Scale (.792), Kutner Morale Scale (.648), and Philadelphia Geriatric Center Morale Scale (.771). Similar intercorrelations were calculated between LSI-B and the above scales. They were .595 for Cavan Adjustment Scale, .883 for Kutner Morale Scale, and .608 for Philadelphia Geriatric Center Morale Scale. The correlation coefficients for LSI-A and LSI-B were .628.

Carp and Carp (1983) compared the LSI-A with several scales and reported the following correlations: .65 with Campbell Index of Overall Well-being, .83 with Cavan Happiness Scale, and .75 with Philadelphia Geriatric Center Scale. Carstensen and Cone (1983) compared the LSI-B with the PGC Morale Scale and reported a correlation of .64 (p<.001).

PROCEDURE USED IN DATA COLLECTION

Local Associations of Indians were contacted by the researcher. A letter was mailed to explain the purpose and nature of the study, and several follow-up calls were made. Additionally, the researcher at various Asian Indian community functions made personal visits for announcements. Announcements seeking volunteers were printed in 'India Globe' newspaper, as well as newsletters of Sri Siva Vishnu Temple, Pranthik, Gujarati Samaj of Washington, and Kerala Association of Greater Washington. Radio announcements were made on the program, "Spirit of India", and several flyers were posted at local Indian grocery stores.

Asian Indian elderly men and women who contacted the researcher for participation were screened to ensure that they met the criteria for selection in this study. While no level of English proficiency was set, none of the respondents indicated difficulty expressing themselves in English. Most interviews were primarily conducted at the homes of respondents. Some interviews were conducted at a temple and at community functions held by various Indian Associations.

All subjects were given an explanation of the study, informed that participation was voluntary, and required to sign a consent form (see Appendix A). Confidentiality was maintained by not using names in the interview or record of responses. The interview began with four open-ended questions, followed by the rest of the interview schedule. This was followed by Life Satisfaction Index-B. Finally, Life Satisfaction Index-A was administered as a paper and pencil questionnaire. On an average, each interview lasted approximately an hour.

DATA ANALYSIS

Quantitative analysis

Research data was examined in several ways. Means and standard deviations of selected socio-demographic and domain variables are presented along with frequencies and percentages. The mean scores of LSI-A and LSI-B are reported along with reference to established norms. In examining sex differences in life satisfaction, a t-test was performed for each item, subscale scores and total scores of the LSI-A and LSI-B.

To test whether socio-demographic factors and domain variables explain variance in life satisfaction among elderly men and women, a series of one-way analysis of variance was performed using subscale and total scores of LSI-A and LSI-B. Pearson's product moment correlation was calculated for all the continuous independent variables and scores on LSI-A and LSI-B.

In order to tease out the effects of self-assessed health, a regression procedure was used to determine if any of the variables found significant by ANOVA could explain any additional variance in life satisfaction. Categorical variables such as sex, marital status, employment, living arrangement, and mode of transportation were dummy coded before being entered into the regression run.

Qualitative analysis

Seven open-ended questions of Life Satisfaction Index -B (LSI-B) as well as four open-ended questions from the devised Interview Schedule were qualitatively analyzed using domain analysis. A domain analysis involves a search for the larger units of cultural knowledge called domains, that include cultural symbols by virtue of some similarity (Spradley, 1980).

In making a domain analysis, the following procedure suggested by Spradley (1980) was employed. For every question analyzed, the first step in making a domain search was to identify the verbatim notes from the interview. The next step was to look for names for things. This involved reading through the notes to look for folk terms that name things as well as nouns.

The third step was to see if any of these folk terms may be cover terms or names for domains, that included other terms or are being used for more than one thing. For example, the cover term "quality of life" included better health facilities, higher standard of living, cleaner air, nourishing food, and so on. Also, the term "quality of life" was used for both physical aspects of the environment (for example, cleaner air) as well as material aspects (for example, standard of living).

The fourth step was to search through the verbatim notes to identify as many included terms as possible. Having done this for one domain, the same process was repeated to find additional domains for the same question. Finally, this entire process was repeated for every open-ended question that was qualitatively analyzed.

IV
Results

The purpose of this study was to explore the level of life satisfaction among immigrant Asian Indian elderly men and women living in the United States and to determine the variables that explain differences in levels of life satisfaction.

LEVEL OF LIFE SATISFACTION

In order to assess the level of life satisfaction among the fifty men and women participants interviewed, Life Satisfaction Index A (LSI-A)and Life Satisfaction Index B (LSI-B) were used. This study demonstrated a positive correlation of .55 (p<.05) between LSI-A and LSI-B (see Table 15). This significant relationship is consistent with earlier findings reported by Lohmann (1977), and Neugarten, Havighurst, and Tobin (1961).

Life Satisfaction Index-A

Results indicate that for Life Satisfaction Index-A, the scores ranged from 6 to 18, within a possible range of 0 to 18. For LSI-A, this sample recorded a mean score of 12.32 (SD=3.02), and this corresponded with the score of 12.4 (SD=4.4) reported by Neugarten, Havighurst, and Tobin (1961).

Life Satisfaction Index-B

Results suggest that for Life Satisfaction Index-B, the scores ranged from 9 to 22, while 23 was the highest possible attainment. In this study, the average score on LSI-B for this sample was 15.94 (SD=2.97). This was marginally higher than the average score of 15.1 (SD=4.7) determined by Neugarten, Havighurst and Tobin (1961).

Open-ended questions of LSI-B

The seven open-ended questions of LSI-B were qualitatively analyzed, using the procedure suggested by Spradley (1980), to elicit rich, descriptive information about those interviewed. Since "life in general" or "life as a whole" is the referent, a long-term perspective is implied. These open-ended questions have a past and or present, or future orientation.

In examining present orientation, respondents were asked, "What are the best things about being the age you are now?" More than half of the elderly men and women interviewed discussed completion of family responsibilities and duties. They included completion of such duties as raising children, educating them, performing their marriages, assisting them with rearing grandchildren, and helping them settle down. As one older respondent replied, "I have more or less successfully completed my obligations to my children. I feel relieved and happy." Family was one of the domains that were identified in the qualitative analysis. Others talked about leisure opportunities as well as fewer stresses compared to earlier periods of their life.

While most respondents discussed completion of family duties and responsibilities to the above question, they did not primarily identify this when asked, "What is the most important thing in your life right now?" In this study, respondents were more likely to isolate maintenance of good health, including their fear of incapacitation and dependency as the most important thing in their life. Health was another domain that was consistently seen across several open-ended questions.

Another secondary response that emerged was mention of the welfare and well being of family members. Again, family members often interlinked this to the maintenance of good health. In other words, older respondents who identified their family as being important, also raised concerns about family members keeping good health and being happy.

To get a flavor for satisfaction with current living situation, respondents were asked to state where they would most like to live, if they could do as they pleased. More than half of the fifty male and female participants mentioned living in the United States as a favored choice. Other choices in order of frequency were living in India, Africa, Japan, Mauritius and France. Since the question was not structured to elicit reasons for choice stated, no further analysis was possible.

In this study, both male and female respondents unanimously denied being worried about their ability to do what others expected of them. A number of respondents indicated that their children, or familymembers really never conveyed anything about what was expected of them. The last question on present orientation aimed to determine whether older respondents had enough time to themselves, or would like to see their friends more often. More than half of the fifty male and female respondents indicated that they would like to see their friends more often than they did.

All respondents were asked to make a comparison of their present period when compared with earlier periods in life. Those who expressed satisfaction with the present period were more likely to discuss completion of family duties and responsibilities. For example, statements such as "Earlier periods were full of duties and responsibilities to family. There is virtually none of that now. Others have fewer expectations and I feel more relaxed and peaceful" were common. On the other hand, those who expressed dissatisfaction with the present period were more likely to talk about loss of good health or death of spouse. As one participant indicated, "Having lost my wife, this is not the best period. Her presence today would have made this a golden period."

In examining future orientation, respondents were asked to discuss any plans for the future. While most respondents stated specific plans, nearly all their responses were qualified. In other words, participants stated their plans for the future to include travel, visit holy shrines, teach, write a book, be with family, and increase community involvement, but nearly all responses were contingent on maintaining good health, *karma*, or the will of God. As one respondent indicated, "There are so many things I would like to do—travel, teach, but only if I enjoy good health." In Hindu culture, *karma* refers to reaping of past deeds, good or bad. Statements such as, "What is the use of my making plans to travel? Who knows if it's in my *karma* to do so?" and "God willing, I would like to be more involved in the local efforts to build a temple here" were quite common.

Open-ended questions (Interview Schedule)

The first question posed to respondents was a general, global question asking participants to comment about their life in America. The elders were asked, "Tell me about life in America." In examining the responses of adult men and women, it was clear that a divergent positive or negative theme emerged as a response to this question. A qualitative assessment of the responses to the four open-ended questions was conducted using Spradley's (1980) procedure for domain analysis. In addition to the earlier domains of family and health, this assessment identified two additional domains. They were positive and negative affect about life in the United States, and cultural differences.

The positive theme about life in America focused on the better quality of life here, including nourishing food, better living conditions, higher standard of living, cleaner air, and excellent health care. As one respondent summed it up, "The living conditions are good here. The food we eat is wholesome, not adulterated like in India. We can be sure of its dietary content. The water supply is well chlorinated, so we don't suffer from illnesses that are water related. The air is quite good, even though there are so many automobiles. There is a lot of greenery and growing importance given to the environment."

About one-third of those interviewed liked the multi-ethnic population of the United States. Those who discussed this issue indicated that they had neighbors who belonged to diverse ethnic groups. As an older respondent stated, "I feel like I know people from all parts of the world. In this street itself, we are five foreigners. Since I baby-sit, I know people from different places. I am always explaining about Indian culture, and exchanging recipes, and household remedies. It is simply terrific."

Nearly half of those who felt positive about life in America, also discussed the value and importance given to privacy and individualism in a favorable light. Most respondents who talked about privacy and individualism also emphasized that these values are not given much consideration in India. As one respondent added, "Instead in India, everyone considers it their right to know what is going on in everyone else's life."

By contrast, those who had negative feelings about life in the United States, talked about feeling restricted and lonely. As respondents indicated, "When all my children are settled here, what other choice but to live here?", and "I think spending the whole day alone when children are working is a form of punishment."

The majority of those who expressed negative sentiment about life here, also talked about the fast pace of life. As one participant put it, "Everyone here is always in a hurry to get to work, to get home, to beat the traffic, to finish groceries, or to get off the phone." A few respondents talked about growing materialism in this society as well as the impact of this on their family. An older respondent said, "My grand-son wants a car to go to school only because all his friends own a car." Some older adults also expressed concerns that their own adult children had begun to espouse values that they could not relate to. Those who mentioned this were more likely to identify assertiveness, individualism, privacy, and materialism as intergenerational barriers within the household.

To examine similarities and differences when compared to other older adults, older male and female respondents were asked to make two kinds of comparisons. First, they were asked to compare their life here with that of older Indians in India. Second, subjects were asked to compare their life with that of older Americans living in the United States.

For the first comparison, approximately half of the fifty men and women interviewed, talked about a better life here compared to older Indians in India. Reasons cited were better living conditions, and a higher standard of living.

The other half felt life was better for older Indians in India. They described the social network in India as more friendly, informal, and casual. These respondents also felt the quality of household care they received here was restricted to weekends. In this context, older respondents talked about their feelings of loneliness, especially when children and their spouses are typically at work. As an older individual responded, "Initially, I could not understand the American accent. I felt Americans talked very fast. I would have the television switched on throughout the day, so I could have the comfort of human voices. I still use television to fight loneliness."

For the second comparison, however, nearly all respondents felt their life here was better than that of older Americans living here. Ethnocentric views regarding family ties and respect for older people were frequently mentioned. As one older respondent said, "The importance given to elderly individuals and family bonds by Indians is shamefully absent in this culture". It was clear from examining several similar responses of older adults that they took pride in the importance given to family in Indian culture, and expressed remorse at the status of older people in American society. As another individual indicated, "Older people are treated here as second-class citizens. In India, most people look up to older people and treat them with respect. This is true even for older people who are complete strangers."

Less than one-third of those interviewed felt they could not compare their lives here with that of older Americans. The reason they cited was that they had not adequately interacted with older Americans to do so. These respondents mentioned differences in food, language, culture, and social systems as barriers for freely interacting with Americans. Cultural differences that were mentioned by respondents were identified as the last domain.

The last open-ended question was a general, global question on satisfaction/dissatisfaction with life. Nearly all respondents reported satisfied rather than dissatisfied with life. This response was similar to the results obtained from the indices of LSI-A and LSI-B, where respondents reported average or higher life satisfaction. Statements such as, "I was able to rear my children into educated people, get them married, and now I am enjoying the last years with them", "I have led a good life, I have no complaints", and "I am proud of all my accomplishments" were commonly echoed by most respondents.

More than half the respondents discussed completion of family responsibilities and satisfaction with having done one's duty. This response was similar to the responses obtained from the open-ended questions of LSI-B.

CASE STUDIES

The case of Mrs. L

Mrs. L has been in the United States since 1981. Widowed in India, unable to manage the household alone, she moved to the United States to be with her adult children. Today, she has five children in the United States, three daughters and two sons. They live in different parts of the United States, though two daughters live within a two-hour drive.

At age 63, Mrs. L left India permanently to be with her children. Her oldest child, "Jay" had sponsored her after she became a citizen of the United States. "Jay" acquired citizenship through marriage to an Asian Indian scientist who was settled in the United States since the mid- 1970s. By acquiring her permanent residency and consequent citizenship, Mrs. L was able to sponsor her other children to relocate to the United States. During this time period, she continued to reside with "Jay" as her family provided short-term support till family members settled down. Over the last decade, all of Mrs. L's children have settled down with decent paying jobs, and are married.

To Mrs. L's disappointment, her older son married a Caucasian. While she admitted that they seem happy, she fretted over the loss of culture and family legacy. She indicated that she did not feel comfortable staying for long in that household. To her satisfaction, her younger son married a girl that was approved by the extended family in India. While Mrs. L hopes to stay permanently with this offspring, she has put her plans on hold for now as they are newly-weds.

Mrs. L receives SSI from the United States Government. This assists her with medical bills, and pocket money for miscellaneous purchases. Lately, she has been moving from one daughter's home to another after staying for about 3-4 months. She stressed that in India, older adults are likely to stay with their sons than daughters. However, her comfort level was much higher with her daughters than her daughters-in-law.

Regarding life in the United States, Mrs. L has mixed feelings. She is happy to be of assistance to her children with babysitting, preparing food, and enjoying some of the comforts of life here. But she was quick to point out that life here is quite lonely. She disliked being dependent on her children for travel to the mall, grocery store, temple, bank, etc. She remarked how her own children are so preoccupied with American values, and are in the "acquiring mode." She felt each weekday is endless and repetitive. While she enjoys good health at present, she is apprehensive of the future.

The case of Mr. R

After retirement from the Government of India service in 1984, Mr. R relocated to the United States with his wife of 38 years. They relocated at the insistence of their only child, a son who is a physician in the

Washington metropolitan area. Prior to this permanent move, Mr and Mrs. R had visited the United States on several short visits. However, within a year of their arrival as immigrants, Mrs. R died unexpectedly of heart failure.

Mr. R dotes on his son's children – two daughters, ages 5 and 7. His daughter-in-law works part-time, and is able to spend considerable time with family members. However, his son has an erratic schedule and is extremely busy with his thriving medical practice. They live in an affluent suburb of Maryland, and enjoy a very high standard of living. Mr. R does not receive any monetary assistance from the United States Government. He quickly asserts that his finances are adequate, and he has simple needs that his son readily responds to. His pension rupees from the Government of India is a paltry sum when converted to dollars. So, Mr. R has begun to engage in philanthropic activities in India with that money.

Mr. R expressed tremendous satisfaction with life in the United States. He pointed out that his wife's death shattered him considerably. She had been his companion for so many years, and attended to his daily routines with care. It was hard to sort out this experience of loss with the relocation experience since they came together quickly. Apart from his grief, Mr. R indicated "this country has been good to me." He reads the newspaper from cover to cover each morning, and apprises family members of the weather each day. He walks a mile each morning, after his breakfast and has met some friendly faces in the neighborhood. Lately, he has been going to the Senior Center and engages in some of their activities. While he is able to converse in English, he pointed out that there are other cultural barriers that dissuade him from going regularly. His network of friends is largely within the Indian community, primarily those of his son's family. Mr. R understands bus routes, and is adept at using the local transport system. He is an avid reader, and visits the public library often.

Mr. R often stressed that he could not live like this in India with his pension money. He spoke of corruption being rampant in India, and that a civil servant who is honest has nowhere to go. He is very impressed with America's standard of living, efficiency, and environmental consciousness. While he plans to visit India with his son's family next year, Mr. R is certain that America is now home.

The case of Mrs. S

Mrs. S lived in the same small town in India for several decades. She had not seen much of India, was largely housebound and participated in household activities. As she had been widowed at a young age with one son, she was forced to live with her brother's family as her husband's family refused to entertain her. Her brother's family was a large one with four children. Consequently, Mrs. S had been an active participant in household activities for her brother's family. She had no monetary backing, and was completely dependent on their goodwill.

When Mrs. S's son, 'Mani' relocated to the United States he first invited her as visitor. During the four month stay here, she visited all the major tourist attractions of the northeastern United States. She was enamored by America, and thought very highly of the efficient nature of this country. When 'Mani' came to India for a subsequent visit five years later, his marriage was arranged within the same community. When Mani's wife was expecting, her parents came over to the United States, and assisted her with her confinement for nearly six months. As their departure drew closer, Mani requested his mother to relocate to the United States as they could use her help with childcare. Being a citizen of the United States, he filed the necessary paperwork and she became an immigrant shortly.

Mrs. S reported that the initial euphoria of living in this nation lasted only a few months. As both her son and daughter-in-law worked full-time jobs, they came home exhausted. As Mrs. S was nearly 65 and had developed arthritis in her right hand, she explained that she would be exhausted by evening. Her grandson was an active toddler, who demanded considerable attention. She often experienced stress when her daughter-in-law would interject on how to care for the child, rejecting Mrs. S's way of upbringing. Besides caring for the toddler, she was expected to have dinner ready, and take care of the laundry chores.

Once her son and daughter-in-law arrived, she would withdraw into the background to give them privacy. Her weekdays were spent within the confines of the four walls of the house. On weekdays, the only human interaction she had was with her son's family or phone calls received in the household. They lived in a middle-class suburb but she had only seen the neighbors, never met them. She repeatedly contrasted the lifestyle here with that of India, especially when talking of social networks. While she spoke English, this was heavily accented and she had not yet acquired the subtleties of American English. She had no monetary resources, and was completely dependent on her son's family.

She expressed tremendous dissatisfaction with her life, reported a feeling of being "trapped", and experienced strained relationships with her son's wife. She had been requested by one of her son's friends to provide baby-sitting service for payment. However, Mani's wife felt other children would mean less attention for her son, and the new house would be messier. Mrs. S had hoped for the financial opportunity, but that passed as soon as it evolved.

Mrs. S would like to return to India as she feels very exploited by her son's family. She indicated that after a lifetime of hardship she had hoped to enjoy the golden years with her grandson. Instead, she continues to work as hard as she did several years ago.

SEX DIFFERENCES IN LIFE SATISFACTION

The second research question that this study asked, "Are there sex differences in levels of life satisfaction among immigrant Asian Indian elderly presently residing in the United States?" is discussed below.

Life Satisfaction Index-A

In this study, the responses of older and women participants of this study were different from each other as well as similar. A t-test analysis of individual items of LSI-A for men and women demonstrated sex differences for four of eighteen items. Similarly, by examining the results of the t-test analysis, it may be surmised that men and women responded similarly on four of eighteen items. Both differences and similarities are discussed below.

In this study, older men and women differed in their responses when asked to comment on the current years of life. They also differed in their report of whether things they do now are as interesting as before, indicate if they feel old and somewhat tired, and to state if they often get down in the dumps compared to others'.

Older male and female participants responded differently when asked to agree/disagree with the statement, "These are the best years of my life." The mean score for women was .44 (SD=.50) and for men .72 (SD=.45), $t(48)$= -2.0, p<.05. In other words, older men were more likely to rate the present period as the best in their lives than the older women.

Older men and women also differed in their responses to the statement, "The things I do are as interesting to me as they ever were." The mean score for women was .64 (SD=.49) and for men .92 (SD=27), $t(48)$= -2.4, p<.05. For the things they did, men were more likely to report their interest level as similar to the past than women were.

More men than women agreed with the statement, "I feel old and somewhat tired." The mean score for women was .36 (SD=.49) and for men was .72 (SD=.45), $t(48)$= -2.6, p<.05. The fourth item of LSI-A that showed sex differences was, "Compared to other people I get down in the dumps often." The mean score for women was .56 (SD=.50) and for men was .92 (SD=.27), $t(48)$= -3.1, p<.05. Contrary to above differences, older men were more likely to report feeling blue than older women were.

Older men and women responded similarly by agreeing with the following statements, "As I grow older, things seem better than I thought they would be", and "I expect some interesting and pleasant things to happen to me in the future." In fact, the mean scores for both items were identical for men and women: .60, and .68, respectively.

Another striking similarity in the responses of older men and women was observed when both sexes disagreed with statements such as, "This is the dreariest time of my life" and "When I think back over my life, I didn't get most of the important things I wanted." For the first statement, the mean score for women (M=.72, SD=.45) was similar, though marginally higher, than the mean score for men (M=.68, SD=.67). However, for the second statement, the mean scores for men and women were identical at .64 (SD=.49).

These findings on similarity between older men and women indicate that members of both sexes were likely to reflect positively on their past, and maintain an outlook that was optimistic of the present and future.

Subscales of LSI-A.

In addition to examining the individual items of LSI-A, the four subscales of LSI-A were examined for sex differences. Using t-test analysis, the responses of older men and women were examined by the four subscales of Mood Tone, Zest versus Apathy, Congruence, and Resolution versus Fortitude.

This analysis disclosed significant sex differences on two of four subscales, namely, Mood Tone and Zest versus apathy. No significant sex differences were found between the mean scores of men and women on the Congruence as well as Resolution versus Fortitude subscales.

On the Mood Tone subscale, the mean score for women was 3.4 (SD=1.6) and for men was 4.5 (SD=1.3), $t(48)= -2.5$, $p<.05$. In this study, older male respondents reported being happier with their lives and taking greater pleasure in what they did than female respondents.

The second subscale of LSI-A that indicated sex differences was Zest versus Apathy subscale. The mean score for women on the Zest versus Apathy subscale was 3.4 (SD=1.4) and for men was 4.4 (SD=1.0), $t(48)= -2.6$, $p<.05$. In other words, older male respondents were more likely to maintain a present and future life orientation that reflected hope and enthusiasm than older women respondents were. Table 11 presents the results of the t-test analysis of subscales of LSI-A for older men and women interviewed.

Table 11

T-test Men & Women on subscales of Life Satisfaction Index A

LSIA	Women (N=25)		Men (N=25)		T-value	Df
	Mean	SD	Mean	SD		
Subscales						
Mood tone	3.4	1.6	4.5	1.3	-2.5*	48
Zest/apathy	3.4	1.4	4.4	1.0	-2.6*	48
Congruence	2.4	.71	2.5	.65	-.41	48
Resolution vs.						
Fortitude	1.8	.57	2.0	.81	-1.0	48

*p<.05

Life Satisfaction Index-B

While the responses of older men and women were similar on certain items of LSI-B, they were different on other items of LSI-B. A t-test analysis of each item of LSI-B for men and women established sex differences for two of twelve items. Similar responses by older men and women participants were noted on two of twelve items.

Responses of older male and female participants differed when asked about future plans as well as satisfaction with way of life. Older men and women responded differently when asked, "What do you think you will be doing five years from now? How do you expect things will be different in your life from the way they are now?" The mean score for women was 1.32 (SD=.55) and for men 1.76 (SD=.43), $t(48)= -3.1$, p<.05. In this study, men were more likely to report no changes as well as specific plans for the future than women were.

For the second item of LSI-B that revealed significant sex difference, "How satisfied would you say you are with your way of life?", the mean score for women was .88 (SD=.52) and for men was 1.20 (SD=.57), $t(48)$= -2.0, p<.05. In other words, men were more likely to report greater satisfaction with life than women were.

Older men and women responded similarly when presented the following questions: "What is the most important thing in your life right now?" and "Do you wish you could see more of your close friends than you do or would you like more time to yourself?" The mean score for men and women was identical for the first question (M=1.4, SD for men =.65, SD for women = .58). Both older men and women indicated that health was their primary concern at present. For the second question, the mean score for women was similar (M=1.20, SD=1.16), but slightly higher than the mean score for men (M=1.16, SD=.62). Older men and women were also likely to indicate that they would like to see their friends more often..

Open-ended questions of LSI-B

Using Spradley's (1980) procedure for domain analysis, the responses to the seven open-ended questions of LSI-B were qualitatively examined for sex differences. No sex differences were observed for most of the open-ended questions of LSI-B.

Men and women responded quite similarly when asked about the best things about their present age, to state the most important thing in their life, and to compare the present period with earlier periods. For these questions, the earlier identified domains of family and health did not demonstrate a sex difference. The majority of male and female respondents denied being worried about their ability to do what others expected of them, and approximately equal number of older men and women indicated that they would like to see their friends more often than they did.

However, using qualitative analysis, the responses of older men and women varied for two of the open-ended questions of LSI-B. First, when asked to state plans for the future, older men were more likely to report specific plans than older women interviewed. Future activities that older men frequently discussed were teaching, travel, and greater community involvement. Women respondents were more likely to talk about travel plans and being with the family. However, by and large, their responses tended to be qualified and dependent on good health, *karma*, or the will of God.

The second question asked respondents to state where they would most like to live, if they could do as they pleased. Of the fifty participants interviewed, more women than men chose the United States. On the other hand, men were more likely to choose other countries such as India, Africa, Japan, Mauritius, and France. As indicated earlier, no further analysis was possible as the question was not structured to elicit reasons for choice made.

Table 12

T-test Men and Women on total scores of Life Satisfaction Index A & B

Women (N=25)		Men (N=25)		T-value Df	
Mean	SD	Mean	SD		
Total Scores					
LSIA	11.16 3.09	13.48	2.50	-2.9*	48
LSIB	15.32 3.15	16.56	2.70	-1.49	48

*p<.05

Total scores of LSI-A & LSI-B

Using t-test analysis, the total scores of LSI-A and LSI-B were scrutinized separately for sex differences. For LSI-A, a two-tailed t-test showed a significant difference between the total scores of women (Mean = 11.16, SD=3.09) and men (Mean=13.48, SD=2.50), $t(48)$= -2.9, p<.05. In this study, men reported significantly higher life satisfaction than women as measured by LSI-A. No such difference was found on LSI-B (see Table 12).

Qualitative assessment

In addition to analysis of LSI-A and LSI-B for sex differences, a qualitative analysis of open-ended questions was carried out. Four open-ended questions from the devised Interview Schedule were qualitatively examined for sex differences.

In describing life in America, the sentiment of "feeling restricted and lonely" was expressed more often by older women than men. As some woman respondents put it, "I am a captive here, but all my children live in America so I have no choice", " There are all kinds of physical comforts in America, but I feel loneliness is a very high price to pay for it."

A number of older women expressed varying sentiments about the difficulties and barriers for older Indians living here. More than half the older women interviewed talked about a sense of isolation, a lack of community feeling in their neighborhood, missing regular attendance at temples, as well as the inability to speak in one's native language.

On the other hand, older men were more likely to report positively about life in the United States. Nearly two-thirds of those older men interviewed discussed the better quality of life in the United States than women. As an older widower said, "There are all comforts of life here. I could never imagine living like this as a retired man". Another man said, "With better health facilities, good food, better living conditions, I have nothing else to ask for."

The positive report given by older male respondents of life in the United States was quite contrary to their stated choice of living situation. As explained earlier, older men were more likely to choose countries other than the United States. On the other hand, despite reporting negative sentiments about life in the United States, women were more likely to express a preference for living in the United States. However, since no reasons for preference indicated was sought, no further analysis was possible.

In examining similarities as well as differences in comparison to other older adults, two kinds of comparisons were sought. For the first comparison, participants were asked to compare their own life here with that of older Indians living in India. In this study, more than half the number of older men interviewed were likely to report that their life here was different and better. Reasons cited for this were better quality of life and higher standard of living. On the other hand, approximately one-third of women respondents reported that their life here was different and worse than that of older respondents living in India. Older women respondents often talked about lacking an adequate social network, feeling lonely, especially when alone at home throughout the day.

For the second comparison, respondents were asked to compare their own life here with that of older Americans living here. Nearly all men and women reported that their own life was better than that of older Americans. Several respondents talked about Indian culture, specifically the importance given to family and the status of older people. There were no sex differences for this comparison. As one respondent put it, "My life is certainly different from that of older Americans. I am a family man. Our Indian culture places so much importance to family. My children are very concerned about me, they take good care of me. Americans are more interested in clubs, parties, and meeting other people. They do not value their family as much as we do."

For the global, general question on life satisfaction, nearly all respondents reported being satisfied rather than dissatisfied with life. This was similar to the finding on level of life satisfaction found in LSI-A and LSI-B, where older men and women reported moderate levels of life satisfaction. However, a qualitative analysis of this item demonstrated no sex differences for this global question from the devised Interview Schedule. This was contrary to the findings of LSI-A where older men reported greater satisfaction than older women on total scores of life satisfaction.

VARIABLES RELATED TO LIFE SATISFACTION

In order to identify the variables that explain differences in level of life satisfaction, a series of one-way ANOVA was performed using total scores of Life Satisfaction Index-A, as well as Life Satisfaction Index-B. While the ANOVA procedure explained whether variables were significant or not, this procedure could not identify which of the response categories, or contrasts for each variable was significantly different. In order to pinpoint which contrasts were significantly different, those variables that were determined significant in explaining differences in level of life satisfaction were further examined by the Tukey Honestly Significant Difference (HSD) test.

Socio-demographic variables

In explaining differences in level of life satisfaction, the following socio-demographic variables were found significant: sex, and reasons for coming to the United States. No difference in degree of life satisfaction expressed by respondents was found for those who differed on age, marital status, employment, education, and length of stay in the United States.

Sex

There is a significant sex difference in reported life satisfaction as measured by LSI-A. The mean scores for men are higher (M=13.48, SD= 2.50) than those reported by women (M=11.16, SD= 3.09) on LSI-A (see Table 11). Using the four subscales of LSI-A, sex differences were further investigated. Results show that there is a significant sex difference for the subscales of Mood Tone and Zest versus Apathy of LSI-A (see Table 12) The mean score on Mood Tone (Mean for Women = 3.44, SD= 1.60; Mean for Men = 4.52, SD= 1.38) and Zest versus Apathy (Mean for Women = 3.48, SD= 1.47; Mean for Men = 4.44; SD= 1.00) show higher reported life satisfaction for men than women. No significant difference in life satisfaction was reported for the subscales of Congruence as well as Resolution versus Fortitude.

Reasons for coming to the United States.

Differences in levels of life satisfaction were noted among respondents who differed on reasons for coming to the United States. A significant difference in life satisfaction was observed between those who came here for family (M=15.34, SD= 2.88) versus 'Other' reasons (M=18.00, SD= 2.69), $F(2, 47)= 4.377$, $p<.05$. The category 'Other' primarily included those who came to the United States via job transfers, diplomat as well as International Organization postings. Those who came to the United States to join family members reported lower levels of life satisfaction than those who came here through job affiliations.

Domain Variables

Living arrangement

The type of housing that respondents reported living in was found to be related to different levels of life satisfaction. This was true for the Index of LSI-B. A significant difference in life satisfaction was reported by those living in an apartment for the elderly (N=3) and those living with non-relatives (N=1). The single respondent living with non-relatives reported significantly greater life satisfaction (M=22.00) than those living in an apartment for the elderly (M=12.00, SD= 3.46), $F(6,43)= 2.36$, $p<.05$.

Another related variable that was found to explain variance in life satisfaction was living relationships. This was reported on the index of LSI-B. Those individuals who reported living alone reported greater satisfaction (M=21.00, SD= 1.41) than those living with spouse (M=14.63, SD= 2.65), $F(3,46)=3.15$, $p<.05$.

Transportation

Results indicate that access to transportation is related to level of life satisfaction as measured by LSI-A. Maximum access to transportation was found related to higher levels of life satisfaction. Those who reported that they had occasional access to transportation reported an average score of 8.00 (SD=1.00) on LSI-A versus an average score of 13.46 (SD=2.78; $F(3,46)=4.73$, $p<.01$) by those who reported that they always had access to transportation.

Self-assessed health

For LSI-A and LSI-B, the personal health rating made by respondents was associated with different levels of life satisfaction. For LSI-A, significant differences were found between those who rated their health as fair (M=9.78, SD= 2.53) versus good (M=13.08, SD= 2.01) or excellent (M=14.33, SD= 2.46), and those who rated their health as poor (M=6.67, SD= 1.15) versus good or excellent. Similarly for LSI-B, the mean score on life satisfaction for those who rated their health as fair was 12.78 (SD= 2.63) as opposed to those who rated their health as good (M=16.68, SD=2.32) or excellent (M=17.50, SD= 2.84). The analysis of variance indicated a significant effect, $F(4, 45)= 11.73$, $p<.01$ (LSI-A) and $F(4, 45)= 6.05$, $p<.01$ (LSI-B) for health rating. This study found better health to be closely associated with greater satisfaction with life.

Again for LSI-A and LSI-B, the results indicate that the evaluation of present health relative to things one would like to do was found related to life satisfaction. For LSI-A, individuals who reported that their health permitted them to do all of the things they wanted to do reported significantly greater life satisfaction (M=14.65, SD= 2.14) than those individuals who said their health limited them to some (M=9.36, SD= 2.46) or most of the things they wanted to do (M=12.42). Similarly, for LSI-B, the average score on life satisfaction for those who said their health allowed them to do all of the things they wanted was 17.59 (SD= 2.37) as opposed to the average scores of 14.07 (SD= 3.26) and 15.84 (SD= 2.47) for those who said their health limited them to some or most of the things they wanted to do. For present health evaluation, the analysis of variance indicated a significant effect, $F(2,47)=21.81$, $p<.01$ (LSI-A) and $F(2,47)= 6.59$, $p<.01$ (LSI-B).

Finance

The reported financial satisfaction of participants was significantly related to life satisfaction on the instrument of LSI-A. Results show significant differences between those who considered their finances adequate (M=11.37, SD= 3.07) and those who considered it more than adequate for their needs (M=13.58, SD= 2.79), $F(2,47)= 3.312$, $p<.05$. Those who reported greater financial adequacy were more likely to report higher levels of life satisfaction.

Social interaction (friends)

The number of friends in the United States that participants reported was associated with life satisfaction as measured by LSI-B. Those who had no friends reported an average score of 12.80 (SD=.44) and those who reported having ten or more friends received an average score of 17.00 (SD= 2.54) on LSI-B, $F(3,46)= 5.28$, $p<.01$. In other words, a large network of friends appear to be related to higher levels of life satisfaction.

In addition to number of friends, the frequency of average number of meetings with friends was also found significant in explaining differences in life satisfaction for the index of LSI-B. Respondents who had no friends to meet scored significantly lower (M=12.80, SD= .44) on life satisfaction than respondents who reported meeting their friends everyday (M=15.00) $F(5,44)= 2.53$, $p<.05$.

Controlled for self-assessed health

Health was strongly correlated with life satisfaction, as measured by both indices of Life Satisfaction Index- A and B. Health rating was significantly correlated with LSI-A ($r=.66$, $p<.01$) and LSI-B ($r= .49$, $p<.01$). Similarly, the correlation between present health evaluation and

LSI-A (r=.69, $p<.01$) as well as between present health evaluation and LSI-B (r= .46, $p<.01$) showed significance.

Since health was identified as strongly correlated to life satisfaction, a further analysis was conducted to see if other independent variables that were found significant by ANOVA, could explain additional variance in life satisfaction, when controlled for self-assessed health (health rating and present health evaluation). In other words, each of these variables were added in after health rating or present health evaluation, to see if there was a significant increment in the variance explained.

Life Satisfaction Index-A

For Life Satisfaction Index-A, the variable, health rating, explained 44% of the variance, and present health evaluation explained 47% of the variance in life satisfaction. When both health rating and present health evaluation were separately controlled for, none of the following variables explained additional, significant variance in life satisfaction: sex, access to transportation, and finance (see Table 13).

Table 13

Summary of predictors of life satisfaction (LSI-A), while controlling for self-assessed health

Variables	Multiple R	R^2	F-change
Health rating	.669	.448	38.97**
Sex	.682	.466	1.57
Finance	.698	.488	3.71
Access to transportation	.684	.468	1.82
Present health evaluation	.690	.476	43.75**
Sex	.710	.505	2.70
Finance	.697	.486	.896
Access to transportation	.699	.489	1.13

**p<.01, *p<.01

Access to transportation, and sex were not significant in explaining additional variance, and this may be explained by the intercorrelation between these variables and health. There is a significant, positive correlation between sex (r=.39, $p<.01$), access to transportation (r=.39, $p<.01$) and health rating. Similarly, the correlation between sex (r=.33, $p<.01$), access to transportation (r=.43, $p<.01$) and present health evaluation is positive and significant. However, no such relationship was found between finance and health rating or present health evaluation.

Life Satisfaction Index-B

On the one hand, for LSI-B, when health rating and present health evaluation were separately controlled, sex, and access to transportation were not identified as significant predictors of life satisfaction in this sample. As indicated above, there was a positive, significant correlation between sex and self-assessed health as well as between access to transportation and self-assessed health.

On the other hand, for LSI-B, variables such as reasons for coming to the United States, number of friends, average meeting with friends, living relationships and type of housing showed significance as contributors in explaining the variance in life satisfaction, when self-assessed health (health rating and present health evaluation) was controlled for (see Table 14).

In addition to the variance explained by health rating (24%) for LSI-B, reasons for coming to the United States explained 14%, number of friends explained 10%, average meeting with friends explained 6%, living relationship explained 9%, and type of housing explained 18% of the variance in life satisfaction and were identified as significant predictors of life satisfaction.

While present health evaluation explained 21% of the variance in LSI-B, the following variables were significant in explaining variance in life satisfaction: reasons for coming to the United States (12%), number of friends, (12%), average meeting with friends (9%), living relationship (11%) and type of housing (23%) (see Table 14).

Table 14

Summary of predictors of life satisfaction (LSI-B), while controlling for self-assessed health

Variables	Multiple R	R^2	F-change
Health rating	497	.247	15.78**
Sex	497	.247	.013
Reasons for coming (USA)	.621	.386	5.199**
Access to tranportation	.499	.249	.110
Type of housing	.653	.426	2.19*
Living relationship	.581	.338	2.05*
Number of friends	.586	.343	6.88*
Average meeting friends	.556	.309	4.25*
Present health evaluation	.468	.219	13.46**
Sex	.471	.222	.207
Reasons for coming (USA)	.579	.335	4.03*
Access to transportation	.470	.221	.135
Type of housing	.663	.440	2.76*
Living relationship	.569	.324	2.34*
Number of friends	.582	.339	8.58**
Average meeting friends	.552	.305	5.83*

**p<.01, *p<.05

V

Conclusions, Discussion, and Implications

Three research questions were formulated for this study of life satisfaction among immigrant Asian Indian elderly. They were proposed to examine the level of life satisfaction, investigate sex differences, and to pinpoint the variables that explain variance in life satisfaction.

SUMMARY OF THE FINDINGS

Compared to the norms established for the indices of LSI-A and LSI-B, the level of life satisfaction reported by this sample of Asian Indian elderly immigrant was moderate. The moderate degree of life satisfaction expressed was consistent for both indices of LSI-A and LSI-B, as well as the global, general question on well-being.

Sex differences in levels of life satisfaction were recorded for LSI-A and LSI-B, as well as the responses to open-ended questions. In general, the older Indian men in this sample were more likely to report higher levels of life satisfaction than older women. The following variables were identified as contributing to the differences in levels of life satisfaction: sex, reasons for coming to the United States, living arrangement, self-assessed health, access to transportation, finance, number of friends, and frequency of average meeting with friends.

Nevertheless, when controlled for self-assessed health, only the following variables were identified as significant contributors to the differences in levels of life satisfaction: reasons for coming to the United States, living arrangement (living relationship and type of housing), number of friends, and average meeting with friends.

CONCLUSIONS

The following conclusions are based on the results of the research study:

1. The life satisfaction of Asian Indian immigrant elderly is comparable, or no different, from that of the sample of American elderly that provided the norms for the indices of LSI-A and LSI-B.

2. Older Asian Indian men have higher levels of life satisfaction than older Asian Indian women do.

3. There is support for (a) socio-demographic variables of sex, and reasons for coming to the United States, and (b) domain variables of self-assessed health, transportation, living arrangement, finance, number of friends and frequency of interactions as factors explaining variation in levels of life satisfaction. Self-assessed health is an important predictor of life satisfaction.

DISCUSSION

A discussion of the results obtained from this study is organized under the following headings: (a) Level of life satisfaction, (b) Sex differences in life satisfaction, and (c) Variables related to life satisfaction.

Level of life satisfaction

In this study, older Asian Indian immigrant men and women reported moderate levels of life satisfaction. Overall, the level of life satisfaction reported by those interviewed is comparable to the established mean for the indices of LSI-A and LSI-B.

In addition to the indices of LSI-A and LSI-B, responses to the general, global question on well-being, "Taking everything into consideration, how would you describe your satisfaction with life?" showed consistency with the above findings of LSI-A and LSI-B. Respondents were more likely to report satisfaction rather than dissatisfaction with life, leading to the conclusion that older Asian Indian immigrants perceive their overall life as satisfying.

As the components of life satisfaction indicate, these individuals reported having an optimistic outlook, maintaining a positive present and future orientation, having a positive acceptance of their past, and accepting personal responsibility for their lives.

In examining their lives, this sample was likely to express an affirmation of the meaningfulness of their lives. Erikson (1968) might label this sample of elderly Asian Indian immigrants as successful agers, for they appear to have achieved what he calls ego integrity. Overall, this group expressed a sense of contentment with their past and present lives, as well as maintained a future orientation.

This is somewhat remarkable, considering that these older respondents faced relocation to a distant setting, far removed from where they spent many decades of their life. In several ways, this new environment was culturally distinct from that of their native homeland. Even in voluntary relocation situations, upon entering a new environment, there is a need for the establishment of homeostasis between the self and the new surroundings (Prager, 1986). Yet, despite the trauma of "uprooting", and the numerous stresses associated with leaving one's homeland and resettling in a new environment, this sample of Asian Indian immigrant elderly respondents still appears to be fairly satisfied with life.

The subjects

The moderate level of life satisfaction reported may be explained by the fact that as a group, these respondents were fairly well educated, reported good health, adequate finances, access to transportation, satisfaction with living arrangements, and a reasonable network of family and friends in the United States.

A majority of them indicated that they lived with their children, and maintained extensive contact with immediate family members. These respondents also took pride in their cultural heritage, especially the importance given to family and older people. This was specially emphasized when comparisons were sought with older American people.

Another possible explanation is that the description that respondents provided of their life in India was not dissimilar to their reported present situation. There was consistency in their descriptions of health, and financial situation.

Even though this study did not attempt to ascertain the nature and level of participation in social activities, it is clear that engagement in certain activities played a role in initial contact and recruitment for participation in this study. Just the fact that all who participated in this study were volunteers and responded to an announcement on the radio, at community functions, to mailed flyers of various community organizations, or to bulletin notices at temples and Indian grocery stores suggests that those in the sample were socially active and engaged. This clearly raises the possibility that participants who volunteered were different from nonvolunteers. Those elderly Asian Indians who did not volunteer may not be as socially active and may not have reported as high life satisfaction as those who volunteered.

In addition, the criteria for subject selection, may themselves have targeted a group of respondents that were likely to be more satisfied. For example, this study was limited to English speaking elderly respondents. As Han (1986) concluded, the inability to speak English was a serious issue for the adjustment of Korean elderly residing in the United States. The greater the language barrier, there is increased isolation, and difficulty with participation in services provided in wider society.

Consequently, the ability to speak English in this culture, opens up several opportunities for social participation that may not be possible for those who face language barriers. In Sikri's (1989) interviews of

Asian Indian elderly, it was summarized that people who spoke English, were educated, and found support for self-expression were more likely to report satisfaction with their lives.

Similarly, this study was restricted to those older respondents who had been in the United States for a minimum of two years. This early period after immigration or early exigency period has been identified as a difficult time, and when social isolation reaches its peak. It is quite possible that those older respondents who are currently in the early exigency period are significantly less satisfied than the sample that was studied.

Hindu views of aging

It is also likely that the Hindu view of aging may have exerted an influence on these respondents. The majority (82%) of respondents in this study indicated that they were Hindus. Three other frequently mentioned religious affiliations were Jainism, Sikhism, and Buddhism. These three religions are considered off-shoots of Hinduism and their basic tenets are widely influenced by Hinduism.

It is possible that *nirmoha* which is a prominent value of the latter Hindu stages of life, provides the older Indian individual with the resource or strength necessary to accept the inevitabilities of life. Another Hindu concept, *karma*, was expressed by several respondents and may have had the same effect. Their responses reflected the inevitability of accepting the fruits of one's past actions. The fundamental idea of *karma* is, "As you sow, so shall you reap." Several references to this concept of *karma* are made in the holy Hindu scripture, *Bhagavad-Gita*. Both concepts may help older Asian Indian respondents maintain an optimistic outlook on life.

Sex differences in Life Satisfaction

Sex differences in the levels of life satisfaction expressed by immigrant Asian Indian elderly men and women were observed. In general, the older men in this study reported higher levels of life satisfaction than older women. This sex difference in level of life satisfaction was consistently seen on the subscales, total scores of LSI-A, as well as the response to one item of LSI-B, "How satisfied would you say you are with your way of life?"

While this finding contradicts several studies that report no sex differences in life satisfaction, this study lends support to earlier studies that show elderly women are less satisfied than elderly men (Spreitzer & Snyder, 1974; Knapp, 1976; Medley, 1976).

Life satisfaction of male respondents

Men were more likely than women to rate the present period as the best in their lives, and report that their interest level was similar to the past were. Also, men reported an optimistic outlook and were likely to maintain a positive orientation of the present and future.

On the other hand, male respondents were more likely to report feeling old and tired than female respondents were. This may be explained by the fact that this sample included men who were likely to be older than women respondents. It is possible that increasing age is linked to the experience of greater levels of tiredness. Further, men were more likely than women to indicate that they get down in the dumps were. However, this is inconsistent and contrary to the above findings where men were more likely to report an upbeat, optimistic outlook.

While no sex differences were observed for the global, general question on well-being, older men and women responded differently when talking about their life in the United States. Men were more likely to be positive when describing their life in the United States. This is consistent with the earlier findings that showed men were more likely to indicate a positive orientation of the present.

Life satisfaction of female respondents

Historically, the roles of Asian Indian women were defined in terms of family obligations and duty. As Tilak (1989) reported, a woman was eulogized as the root and support of the family. Even in the early twentieth century, which is the period that most of these respondents grew up in, women were expected to stay within the domestic sphere, and were less encouraged to participate in education, employment, or other non-kinship groups.

In looking at some of the descriptive statistics of this study, it is possible that one or a combination of these variables may explain sex differences in life satisfaction. Less likely to be educated and employed, it is possible that the older women in this study had devoted most of their energies to the family. Now that most of their familial responsibilities and duties were complete, it may be likely that some of the older women experienced lower levels of life satisfaction.

Education, as pointed out by Kiefer et al. (1985), increases an individual's repertoire of available coping strategies. Older women participants were less likely to be educated and employed, and were possibly encouraged to interact within the confines of their kinship circle. Consequently, they may lack the skills and resources that are necessary to adapt to an unfamiliar environment.

Older women respondents were more likely to express feelings of restrictedness, loneliness, and comment on the absence of a sense of community. The following statistics may offer some insights. In this study, women were more likely to indicate that they have no friends and fewer family members than men do. However, these women were likely to meet more frequently with family members than men. It is possible that such frequent interactions with family members are not necessarily positive and rewarding. Instead, such interactions may have an adverse influence on the life satisfaction of these older women.

Further, the women in this study were more likely to assess their health in an unfavorable light, and see it as a limiting factor in some of the things they wanted to do. This in turn, may have directly influenced their satisfaction with life, or indirectly, as they may have been less mobile, functional, or socially active.

VARIABLES RELATED TO LIFE SATISFACTION

Sex

Sex differences in the level of life satisfaction were noted, and this variable was significant in explaining the variance in life satisfaction.

However, when controlled for self-assessed health, sex was not identified as a significant predictor of life satisfaction. In other words, while sex explains differences in the level of life satisfaction, it does not do so when the effects of health are teased out. This points to a relationship between sex and health.

As the results indicate, there is a positive, significant relationship between sex and self-assessed health. It is possible that real sex differences exist between men and women in terms of physical health. This may be consistent with the findings of Verbrugge (1976), who reported that health statistics indicate women have higher illness rates than men.

Reasons for coming to the United States

Reasons for coming to the United States, was determined as an important predictor in explaining variance in life satisfaction. Those respondents who came to the United States for job related reasons reported significantly greater satisfaction than those who came here to be with family members did.

As Kuo and Tsai (1986) explained, under present immigration laws in the United States, the majority of immigrants are admitted either to effect family reunification, or because they possess professional or technical skills. They reported that immigrants in the latter group—that is, professionals and skilled workers, are more likely to find stable employment easier. This, in turn, may help them experience greater levels of security, social acceptance and integration, which may influence their satisfaction with life.

On the other hand, those immigrants who came here to join family members, may have a different set of expectations from family members than those who came here through job affiliations. It is possible that the nature of their social network was inadequate to meet adaptation needs and immigration goals (Kuo & Tsai, 1986).

Domain variables

The results of this investigation suggest that the following domain variables were identified as important in explaining the difference in levels of life satisfaction: living arrangement (type of housing and living relationships), self-assessed health (health rating and present health evaluation), access to transportation, finance, number of friends, and frequency of average meeting with friends.

Health played a leading role in satisfaction with life by accounting for major variance. When controlled for self-assessed health (health rating and present health evaluation), only the following domain variables were identified as explaining additional variance in life satisfaction: living arrangement (living relationship and type of housing), number of friends, and average meeting with friends.

Self-assessed health

The most compelling explanation for variations that have been reported in life satisfaction may be attributed to self-assessed health. In this study, maintenance of good health was closely associated with higher levels of satisfaction with life. Consequently, those who expressed dissatisfaction with life were also likely to report loss of good health. Health as a significant predictor of well-being is consistent with several studies that have highlighted the importance of this variable (Allan & Brotman 1982; Davis, 1982; Quinn, 1980; George & Landerman, 1984).

Health is a basic concern for the elderly (Butler, 1975; Larson, 1978). As a person grows older, there is a gradual, increasing risk of illness and impairment in functioning. Respondents in the present study expressed the importance of health in their lives, including their fear of incapacitation and dependency. No doubt, health plays a vital role and can influence satisfaction with life.

There are diverse ways how health can affect the life of the elderly. Good health implies that individuals have the physical resources to accomplish what they want. When older people are healthy, they are likely to be employed, mobile, functional, and socially active. In other words, the influence of health on life satisfaction is not simply the direct effect of how people feel physically, but also what their health permits them to do.

Living arrangement

The findings of this study suggest that type of housing is an important influence on the level of life satisfaction. This was found true even when self-assessed health was controlled for. In this study, those living in an apartment for the elderly were significantly less satisfied than those individuals who reported living with non-relatives. However, given that only one individual lived with non-relatives, and three individuals lived in an apartment for the elderly, it is not possible to seriously consider this result. It is possible that those individuals living in an apartment for the elderly lack the social/support system or are unfamiliar with how to operate in their novel setting, and consequently less satisfied.

In an interview for the newspaper, 'India Abroad', Mehta (1989), Social Worker and Director of Social Services in Los Angeles, examined the option of day care for Asian Indian immigrant elderly. Mehta (1989) said "I think it may be too much for many parents to leave their kith and kin and live in seniors' home..."

The Hindu system of family obligations prescribes that children should look after their older parents (Ross, 1970). However, in this study, only about half (56%) of the respondents that were interviewed indicated that they were living with their children. This undoubtedly confirms the idea that the traditional, extended family arrangement is gradually changing. The notion that Asian Americans are cared for by their family is perpetuated because of the emphasis on filial piety. However, Kuntz (1997) highlighted the importance of financial and social factors. Elderly Asian Americans who live away from their children, whose adult children lack financial resources, and who are isolated from family and friends may benefit from outside sources. Practitioners should not assume filial obligations is a high priority with adult children. One should assess each case carefully for economic and social factors.

Considering the largely prevailing patrifocal tilt in India, what was noteworthy is that this sample of older immigrants were likely to live with their daughter as much as their son. This is a departure from traditional Hindu society where the married daughter is considered *paraaya dan* (literally, 'outside wealth') or part of her husband's family. It is not uncommon in certain parts of India for parents to largely refrain from paying extended visits with their married daughter.

In addition to the type of housing that respondents lived in, there was a significant difference in life satisfaction based on living relationships. This was found to be a significant predictor, even when self-assessed health was controlled for. Individuals living alone reported greater satisfaction than those living with spouse did. It is possible that since the retirement of this sample and or their married spouse, respondents were spending greater amount of time with their spouses. This often calls for an adjustment, and could, in turn, influence satisfaction with life. This finding supports the work of Depner and Ingersoll-Dayton (1985), who examined conjugal support in later life, and reported that with increasing age, older adults provided their spouses with less support. Again, this finding must be cautiously reported as only two individuals reported living alone.

Transportation

Older respondents using different modes of transportation reported no significant difference in life satisfaction. On the other hand, those who reported limited access to transportation were significantly less satisfied than those who had greater access were.

Having easy access to transportation ensures mobility, and provides greater freedom and choice. Research indicates that well-being is linked with various aspects of living situations, and access to transportation is one of them (Cutler, 1975; Chan, 1988; Skolgund, 1986; Han, 1986). Gelwicks (1974) suggested that a well-developed transport system would ensure that elderly people could maintain access to, and harmony with the world around them.

However, when controlled for self-assessed health, access to transportation was not significant in explaining the variance in life satisfaction. As indicated by the correlation, the two variables are related. Those who enjoy good health are more likely to be physically active, mobile, and seek transportation than those whose health is restrictive.

Finance

A significant difference in life satisfaction was found when assessing financial satisfaction relative to one's needs. Those who reported greater finances relative to needs were more likely to indicate greater satisfaction with life.

Having a strong financial position, provides greater independence and choice with regard to necessary products of living and services. This supports the work of Usui, Keil and Durig (1985), who reported that one's relative financial situation is a significant influence on the life satisfaction of elderly adults.

However, when controlled for self-assessed health, finance was not significant in explaining any additional variance in life satisfaction. Since no significant correlation was found between finance and self-assessed health, it does not point to a relation between the two variables.

Social interaction (friends)

A significant relationship between life satisfaction and number of friends as well as between frequency of average meetings with friends was reported. Even when controlled for self-assessed health, these two variables were found significant in explaining the difference in level of life satisfaction. In other words, personal interactions with greater number of friends are important in providing the elderly with a high level of life satisfaction.

Extrapolating from Arling's work (1976), it may be reasoned that having a number of friends may in itself be rewarding as it opens up opportunities for social interactions. The relation between social interaction with friends and life satisfaction is similar to that reported by Burgio (1987) and Skolgund (1986).

Social interaction (family)

Contrary findings of the relationship between family interaction and life satisfaction were found. Even though the elders talked a lot about family, and often in a positive light, this variable was not significant in explaining the variance in life satisfaction. This may be explained by the fact that in a face to face interview situation, it is socially approved for respondents to be less open in expressing themselves than on a questionnaire such as Life Satisfaction Index-A.

Or perhaps this raises questions about the myth that Asian-American aged are well-cared for in their close kinship system based on culture. Is it possible that these older respondents have become more peer centered and less family oriented since immigration? Or does the process of immigration itself demand that individuals extend their social network to include non-family members as well?

RECOMMENDATIONS AND IMPLICATIONS

Future research

As described earlier, health is clearly a strong predictor of life satisfaction for older respondents of this study. In addition to using self-ratings of health, a report of the nature of health difficulties that respondents may experience would be valuable. This would provide information about the prevalence of health disorders among various groups of older respondents.

Investigating sex differences are an important aspect of assessing life satisfaction. In this study, men and women reported varying levels of life satisfaction. A future study could separately examine the variables that contribute to life satisfaction of older men and women.

Work provides one of the strongest structural supports for integrating an individual into society. Results indicate that coming to the United States through work affiliations was related to higher levels of satisfaction with life. A closer examination of work, its' role and nature is recommended. Such a study may be conducted for individuals of all ages to emphasize the relation between work and life satisfaction for immigrants.

Additional questions are recommended for assessing the relation between finance and life satisfaction. It is suggested that future studies include an assessment of the range of income, as well as sources of income for respondents. Similarly, in studying the association between transportation and life satisfaction, it is advocated that such issues of transportation as availability, safety, and cost are taken into consideration. This will provide a more comprehensive picture of the daily life-style of respondents.

This study was limited to Asian Indian immigrant elderly respondents residing in the Washington Metropolitan area. It may be worthwhile to include a broader geographic distribution to get a sample of older adults from various communities within the United States. Further, increasing the sample size to include Asian Indian elderly respondents from several metropolitan cities, would help increase the generalizability of the findings.

A similar study that examines life satisfaction between various immigrant groups settled in the United States may shed some light on similarities and differences between the experiences of older immigrants. In particular, it is recommended that such comparisons take place with ethnic Asian control groups, whose cultural values are not dissimilar to that of Asian Indians.

As the age and population of Asian Indian immigrants increases, it is advocated that future research be conducted for the children of present-day older immigrants, as they grow older and reach age sixty. This would provide important information on cultural continuity of this cohort that has spent a substantial portion of their lives in the United States as opposed to India.

Gerontological practice

Health

The fact that concern for health was paramount, has implications for health care professionals that provide care for the elderly. The health needs of older people have to be among the primary considerations in any program that is directed at improving the lives of older people.

Increased nutritional knowledge and periodic physical check-ups, will go far toward helping older people maintain strength and health into the later years.Interventions may be directed at managing diet, exercise, medications, so as to promote physical well-being. Further, providing information on health issues is vital to recognize early signs and symptoms of disease.

It is strongly recommended that medical doctors of the Asian Indian community participate in such health maintenance and intervention activities. They may be better able to understand the food habits, language, and daily life style of older respondents. Consequently, these older adults may feel more comfortable relating to them.

Directory

The results of this study also lead to a number of suggestions for service delivery to elderly immigrant populations. First, a directory of of Asian Indian community organizations could be compiled that offer services to older adults. Given that interaction with friends is related to increased life satisfaction, such a directory would help the community of older Asian Indians in myriad ways. This would provide them the resources to locate other seniors in the metropolitan area, create and foster a social network of Asian Indian elderly, and develop programs that would ensure the participation of all elders.

Further, such a directory may help identify elderly immigrants who may benefit from being informed about a variety of programs such as discussion or support groups. Special emphasis may be placed on providing information on housing opportunities, health insurance options, transportation facilities, financial discounts offered for Seniors, and additional resources for building social networks. In addition to the above, such a directory would be a valuable resource for future investigators to conduct further research.

Housing

Since there is a gradual trend towards living independently, Asian Indian community leaders may want to seriously consider providing an option of community housing for the elderly. Such shared housing can offer older respondents the opportunity to speak in their native language, eat Indian food, celebrate Indian festivals and holidays, interact with others from a similar background, and learn ways of dealing with the new culture they are in.

This exploratory research was valuable in developing a preliminary data base of information about Asian Indian immigrant elderly in the United States. It is suggested that programs and policies directed to this group consider this information, so that informed decisions can be made.

Appendix A

Interview Schedule

Open-ended questions

1. Tell me about life in America
2. Compared to older people in India, in what ways is your life different or similar?
3. Compared to older Americans, in what ways is your life different or similar?
4. Taking everything into consideration, how would you describe your satisfaction with life?

Socio-demographic characteristics

1. Gender
   1_____male
   2_____female

2. How old are you? _____years

3. What is your present marital status?
   1. single
   2. married (living with spouse)
   3. divorced
   4. separated
   5. widowed

4. What is the highest education level completed by you?
   1. less than high school graduate
   2. high school graduate
   3. attended college (1-3 years)
   4. completed college
   5. graduate degree or professional training

5. What is your religious belief system? Are you
   1. Hindu
   2. Muslim
   3. Christian
   4. Buddhist
   5. Jain
   6. Sikh
   7. Other (please state) _____

6. Are you presently employed outside the home?
   1. No
   2. Yes

7. If yes, how many hours do you work per week? _____ hours

8. What is the nature of your work?

9. Now, I am going to ask you some questions about household activities. Please respond 'yes' or 'no.' (For every 'yes', ask respondent frequency – How often do you engage in these activities? Is this daily, weekly, fortnightly, or monthly? (circle response)

a. babysitting grandchild/grandchildren	D	W	F	M
b. babysitting other children	D	W	F	M
c. cooking and preparing meals	D	W	F	M
d. doing laundry	D	W	F	M
e. yard work/gardening	D	W	F	M
f. washing dishes/household cleaning	D	W	F	M
g. providing rides	D	W	F	M
h. running errands	D	W	F	M

10. Why did you come to the United States (check all that apply)
    1. economic reasons
    2. political reasons
    3. marriage to an American
    4. to join family members
    5. other (please describe)

11. Who made the decision to come to the United States?
    1. self
    2. spouse
    3. self and spouse
    4. child/children
    5. other (describe)

12. To what extent were you involved in the decision process?
    1. not at all
    2. somewhat
    3. completely

13. How happy were you with the decision at that time?
    1. very unhappy
    2. somewhat unhappy
    3. neither unhappy nor happy
    4. somewhat happy
    5. very happy

14. How many years have you been in the United States? ____years

15. How many years did you live in India? ____years

16. Have you lived in any other country besides India and the United States? If yes, when and for how long?

17. Since your permanent residence in the United States, how often have you been back to India, and for how long?

Domain variables

18. Please describe your current living arrangement. Are you
    1. living alone
    2. living with spouse
    3. living with children
    4. living with grandchildren
    5. living with relatives
    6. living with non-relatives
    7. other (please describe)

19. If you had a choice, would you choose an alternate arrangement?
    1. No
    2. Yes (describe)

20. Where do you live?
    1. my own house/apartment
    2. rented house/apartment
    3. child's home
    4. child's apartment
    5. apartment for the elderly
    6. nursing home
    7. relative's home
    8. non-relative's home

21. What is your usual mode of transportation when you need to go somewhere?
    1. walk
    2. by own car
    3. borrow car
    4. by taxi
    5. take public transportation
    6. ride with others
    7. other (specify)
    8. don't go out at all

22. Do you have access to transportation that will enable you to get to places that you would like to visit?
    1. rarely
    2. sometimes
    3. often
    4. always

23. How would you describe your health in general? Is it
    1. very poor
    2. poor
    3. fair
    4. good
    5. excellent

24. Does your present state of health allow you to
    1. do none of the things you want to
    2. do some of the things you want to
    3. do most of the things you want to
    4. do all of the things you want to

25. As far as your present financial situation is concerned, would you describe this as
    1. less than adequate for your needs
    2. adequate for your needs
    3. more than adequate for your needs

26. Do you have any family members living in the United States?
    1. No (proceed to question #27)
    2. Yes

If yes, please tell me who they are? For each of the following endorsed categories, ask the following questions:

   How many? Using the following scale, indicate on an average, how often do you meet them? Similarly, using the same scale, indicate on an average, how often do you talk or correspond with them?

    1. less than once a year
    2. few times a year
    3. once or twice a month
    4. about once a week
    5. everyday

Family	# of them	Freq of meeting	Freq of talk/correspondence
Child	_____	_____	_____
Child	_____	_____	_____
Child	_____	_____	_____
Child	_____	_____	_____
Child	_____	_____	_____
Grandchild	_____	_____	_____
Grandchild	_____	_____	_____
Grandchild	_____	_____	_____
Grandchild	_____	_____	_____
Grandchild	_____	_____	_____

Sibling	_____	_____	_____
Sibling	_____	_____	_____
Sibling	_____	_____	_____
Sibling	_____	_____	_____
Sibling	_____	_____	_____
Cousin	_____	_____	_____
Cousin	_____	_____	_____
Cousin	_____	_____	_____
Cousin	_____	_____	_____
Cousin	_____	_____	_____
Nephew/ Niece	_____	_____	_____
Nephew/ Niece	_____	_____	_____
Nephew/ Niece	_____	_____	_____
Nephew/ Niece	_____	_____	_____
Nephew/ Niece	_____	_____	_____

27. Do you have any family members living in India?
    3. No (proceed to question #27)
    4. Yes
If yes, please tell me who they are? For each of the following endorsed categories, ask the following questions:
     How many? Using the following scale, indicate on an average, how often do you meet them? Similarly, using the same scale, indicate on an average, how often do you talk or correspond with them?

     6. less than once a year
     7. few times a year
     8. once or twice a month
     9. about once a week
    10. everyday

Family	# of them	Freq of meeting	Freq of talk/correspondence
Child	_____	_____	_____
Child	_____	_____	_____
Child	_____	_____	_____
Child	_____	_____	_____
Child	_____	_____	_____
Grandchild	_____	_____	_____
Grandchild	_____	_____	_____
Grandchild	_____	_____	_____
Grandchild	_____	_____	_____
Grandchild	_____	_____	_____
Sibling	_____	_____	_____
Sibling	_____	_____	_____
Sibling	_____	_____	_____
Sibling	_____	_____	_____
Sibling	_____	_____	_____
Cousin	_____	_____	_____
Cousin	_____	_____	_____
Cousin	_____	_____	_____
Cousin	_____	_____	_____
Cousin	_____	_____	_____
Nephew/ Niece	_____	_____	_____
Nephew/ Niece	_____	_____	_____
Nephew/ Niece	_____	_____	_____
Nephew/ Niece	_____	_____	_____
Nephew/ Niece	_____	_____	_____

28. How many people that you can friends are in the United States?
    1. none
    2. one to four
    3. five to ten
    4. ten or more

29. On an average, how often do you meet them?
    1. not applicable (no friends)
    2. less than once a year
    3. few times a year
    4. once or twice a month
    5. about once a week
    6. everyday

30. On an average, how often do you talk/correspond with them?
    1. not applicable (no friends)
    2. less than once a year
    3. few times a year
    4. once or twice a month
    5. about once a week
    6. everyday

Life in India

31. Which part of India are you from? _____

32. Would you describe this place as
    1. urban/metropolitan
    2. rural/farmland
    3. small town
    4. suburban

33. Please describe your living arrangement in India. Were you
    1. living alone?
    2. living with spouse?
    3. living with children?
    4. living with grandchildren?
    5. living with relatives?
    6. living with non-relatives?
    7. other (please describe)?

34   In India, were you employed outside the home?
   1   No
   2   Yes

If yes, how many hours do you work per week? _____ hours

35   What is the nature of your work?

36   How would you describe your health in India?
   1   very poor
   2   poor
   3   fair
   4   good
   5   excellent

37   As far as your financial situation in India was concerned, would
   you describe this as
   1   less than adequate for your needs
   2   adequate for your needs
   3   more than adequate for your needs

38   In India, what was your usual mode of transportation when
   you needed to go somewhere?
   1   walk
   2   by own car
   3   borrow car
   4   by taxi
   5   take public transportation
   6   ride with others
   7   other (specify)
   8   didn't go out at all

39   Did you have access to transportation that enabled you to get to
   places that you would like to visit?
   1   rarely
   2   sometimes
   3   often
   4   always

40 When living in India, did you have family members there?
　1　No (proceed to question #27)
　2　Yes
If yes, please tell me who they are? For each of the following endorsed categories, ask the following questions:

　　How many? Using the following scale, indicate on an average, how often do you meet them? Similarly, using the same scale, indicate on an average, how often do you talk or correspond with them?

　　　　1　less than once a year
　　　　2　few times a year
　　　　3　once or twice a month
　　　　4　about once a week
　　　　5　everyday

Family	# of them	Freq of meeting	Freq of talk/correspondence
Child	_____	_____	_____
Child	_____	_____	_____
Child	_____	_____	_____
Child	_____	_____	_____
Child	_____	_____	_____
Grandchild	_____	_____	_____
Grandchild	_____	_____	_____
Grandchild	_____	_____	_____
Grandchild	_____	_____	_____
Grandchild	_____	_____	_____
Sibling	_____	_____	_____
Sibling	_____	_____	_____
Sibling	_____	_____	_____
Sibling	_____	_____	_____
Sibling	_____	_____	_____
Cousin	_____	_____	_____
Cousin	_____	_____	_____
Cousin	_____	_____	_____
Cousin	_____	_____	_____
Cousin	_____	_____	_____

Nephew/			
Niece	_____	_____	_____
Nephew/			
Niece	_____	_____	_____
Nephew/			
Niece	_____	_____	_____
Nephew/			
Niece	_____	_____	_____
Nephew/			
Niece	_____	_____	_____

41 How many people that you can friends were in India?
    1   none
    2   one to four
    3   five to ten
    4   ten or more

42 On an average, how often did you meet them?
    1   not applicable (no friends)
    2   less than once a year
    3   few times a year
    4   once or twice a month
    5   about once a week
    6   everyday

43 On an average, how often did you talk/correspond with them?
    1   not applicable (no friends)
    2   less than once a year
    3   few times a year
    4   once or twice a month
    5   about once a week
    6   everyday

Bibliography

Adams, D.L. 1969. Analysis of a Life Satisfaction Index. *Journal of Gerontology* 24(4): 470-474.

Adams, D.L. 1971. Correlates of life satisfaction among the elderly. *Gerontologist* 11(4): 64-68.

Allan, C., and Brotman, H. 1982. *Chartbook on aging in America*. Washington, D.C: 1981 White House Conference.

Andrews, F.M., and Withey, S.B. 1976. *Social indicators of well-being: Americans' perception of life quality*. New York: Plenum.

Archbold, P.G. 1982. All-consuming activity: The family as caregiver. *Generations* 7(2):12-13

Arling, G. 1976. The elderly widow and her family, neighbors, and friends. *Journal of Marriage and Family* 38: 757-768.

Atchley, R. 1980. *The social forces of later life*. Belmont, CA: Wadsworth Publishing Co.

Atchley, R.C. 1982. The aging self. *Psychotherapy: Theory, Research and Practice*, 19: 388-396.

Banchevska, R. 1978. The immigrant family. In J. Krupinski & A. Stoller (Eds.), *The family in Australia*. Elmsford, NY: Pergamon Press.

Bearon, L.B. 1989. No great expectations: The underpinnings of life satisfaction for older women. *The Gerontologist* 29:772-778.

Berghorn, F.J., and Schaefer, D.E. 1981. The quality of life and older people. In F.J. Berghorn & D.E. Schaefer (Eds.), *The dynamics of aging* (pp. 331-351). Boulder, Colorado: Westview Press.

Blau, Z.S. 1981. *Aging in a changing society.* New York: Franklin Watts.

Bultena, G. L., amd Oyler, R. 1971. Effects of health on disengagement and morale. *Aging and human development* 2(2):142-147.

Burgio, M.R. 1987. Friendship patterns and friendship expectancies among the successful aging. *Dissertation Abstracts International,* 48:2424. (University Microfilms No. 8720109)

Campbell, A. 1981. *The sense of well-being in America: recent patterns and trends.* New York: McGraw Hill.

Campbell, A., Converse, P., and Rodgers, W. 1976. *The quality of American life: perceptions, evaluations, and satisfactions.* New York: Russell Sage Foundation.

Carp, F., and Carp, A. 1983. Structural stability of well- being factors across age and gender, and development of scales of well-being unbaised for age and gender. *Journal of Gerontology* 38:572-581.

Carstensen, L., and Cone, J. 1983. Social desirability and the measurement of psychological well-being in elderly persons. *Journal of Gerontology* 38:713-715.

Cavan, R. S., Burgess, E. W., Havighurst, R. J., and Goldhammer, H. 1949. *Personal adjustment in old age.* Chicago: Science Research Associates.

Chan, F. 1988. To be old and Asian: an unsettled life in America. *Aging* 358: 14-15.

Chou, R.J. 1987. Health and sociocultural factors related to life satisfaction: A study of the elderly in Oakland's Chinese community. *Dissertation Abstracts International* 49:535. (University Microfilms No. 8806212)

Cicirelli, V.G. 1981. *Helping elderly parents: The role of adult children.* Boston, MA: Auburn House.

Clark, M. and Anderson, B. 1967. *Culture and Aging.* Springfield, IL: Charles C. Thomas.

Cockerham, W. 1983. Aging and perceived health status. *Journal of Gerontology* 38(3): 349-355.

Coelho, G., Ahmed, P., and Yuan, Y. 1980. *Uprooting and development.* New York: Plenum Press.

Collette, J. 1984. Sex differences in life satisfaction: Australian data. *Journal of Gerontology* 39(2):243- 245.

Conner, K., Powers, E., and Bultena, G. 1979. Social interaction and Life Satisfaction: An empirical assessment of late-life patterns. *Journal of Gerontology* 34(1): 116-121.

Conte, V., and Salamon, M. 1982. An objective approach to the measurement and use of Life satisfaction with Older persons. *Measurement and evaluation in Guidance* 15(3):194-200.

Cowgill, D.O. 1986. *Aging around the world.* Belmont, CA: Wadsworth Publishing Company.

Crandall, R.C. 1980. *Gerontology: A behavioral approach.* Reading, MA: Addison-Wesley.

Cumming, E., and Henry, W. 1961. *Growing old: A view in depth of the social and psychological processes in aging.* New York: Basic Book.

Cutler, N.E. 1981. Voluntary association participation and life satisfaction: replication, revision, and extension. *International Journal of Aging and Human Development* 14:127-137.

Cutler, S. 1973. Volunteer association participation and life satisfaction: a cautionary research note. *Journal of Gerontology* 28:96-100.

Cutler, S. 1975. Transportation and changes in life satisfaction. *Gerontologist* 15:155-159.

Davis, J. 1981. *General Social Surveys 1972-1980, Cummell Codebook.* Chicago: National Opinion Research Center.

Depner, C., and Ingersoll-Dayton, B. (1985). Conjugal social support: Patterns in later life. *Journal of Gerontology* 40(6): 761-766.

Desai, M.M. and Khetani, M.D. 1979. Intervention strategies for the aged in India. In M. Teicher, D. Thursz, & J. Vigilante (Eds.), *Reaching the aged.* Beverly Hills: Sage Publications.

Diener, E. 1984. Subjective well-being. *Psychological Bulletin* 3: 542-575.

Dowd, J.J. 1981. Aging as exchange: A preface to theory. In C.S. Kart & B.B. Manard (Eds.), *Aging in America: Readings in Social Gerontology,* pp. 58-71. Palo Alto, CA: Mayfield.

Edwards, J., and Klemmack, D. 1973. Correlates of life satisfaction: a reexamination. *Journal of Gerontology* 28: 497-502.

Erikson, E. 1959. Identity and the life cycle: Selected papers. *Psychological Issue Monograph Series, 1.* New York: International Universities Press.

Erikson, E. 1969. *Gandhi's truth.* New York: Norton.

Eu, H. 1987. An exploratory study of the correlates of life satisfaction among the Korean elderly. *Masters Abstracts International* 26:204.

Faucher, T.A. 1979. Life satisfaction among elderly women in three living arrangements. *Dissertation Abstracts International*, 40/05B:2431.

Fawcett, G., Stonner, D., and Zepelin, H. (1980). Locus of control, perceived constraint, and morale among institutionalized aged. *International Journal of Aging and Human Development* 11:13-23.

Fengler, A.P., and Jensen, L. 1981. Perceived and objective conditions as predictors of the life satisfaction of urban and nonurban elderly. *Journal of Gerontology* 36:750-752.

Fengler, A.P., Little, V.C., and Danigelis, N.L. 1983. Correlates of dimensions of happiness in urban and nonurban settings. *International Journal of Aging and Human Development* 16:53-65.

Ferraro, K.F. 1980. Self-ratings of health among the old and the old-old. *Journal of Health and Social Behavior* 21: 377-383.

Fischer, D.H. 1979. *Growing old in America* (2nd edition). London: Oxford University Press.

Fitinger, L., and Schwartz, D. 1981. *Strangers in the World*. Bern: Hans Huber.

Fletcher, C.N., and Lorenz, F.O. 1985. Structural influences on the relationship between objective and subjective indicators of economic well-being. *Social Indicators Research* 16:333- 345.

George, L.K. 1979. The happiness syndrome: Methodological and Substantive issues in the study of social- psychological well-being in adulthood. *Gerontologist* 2:210-216.

George, L.K., and Bearon, L.B. 1980. *Quality of life in older persons: Meaning and measurement* New York: Human Science Press.

George, L. 1981. Subjective well-being: conceptual and methodological issues. In C. Eisdorfer (Ed.), *Annual Review of Gerontology and Geriatrics* 345-382. New York: Springer Publ.

George, L.K., and Landerman, R. 1984. Health and subjective well-being: A replicated secondary data analysis. *International Journal of Aging and Human Development* 19:133-156.

Gibson, R.C. 1989. Minority aging research: opportunity and challenge. *Journal of Gerontology* 44: 2-3.

Glenn, N. 1975. The contribution of marriage to the psychological well-being of males and females. *Journal of Marriage and the Family* 37:594-600.

Gore, M.S. 1978. *Urbanization and family change.* Bombay: Popular Prakashan.

Gottlieb, G.H. 1983. *Social support strategies: Guidelines for Mental health practice.* Beverly Hills: Sage Publications.

Grafje, R.F. 1984. The decomposition of the relationship between selected demographic factors, personality characteristics, and life satisfaction among the elderly. *Dissertation Abstracts International* 45:2711. (University Microfilms No. 8423123)

Graney, M.J., and Zimmerman, R.M. 1980. Causes and consequences of health self report variations among older people. *International Journal of Aging and Human Development* 12:292-300.

Grarey, M. J. 1975. Happiness and social participation in aging. *Journal of Gerontology* 30:701-706.

Han, M. S. 1986. Social interaction and life satisfaction among the Korean-American elderly (United States). *Dissertation Abstracts International* 47: 10A.

Havighurst, R., Neugarten, B., and Tobin, S. 1968. Disengagement and patterns of aging. In B.N. Neugarten (Ed.), *Middle age and aging.* Chicago: University of Chicago press.

Havighurst, R. 1972. *Developmental tasks in education* (3rd edition). New York: David McKay Company Inc.

Hess, B.B., and Markson E.W. 1980. *Aging and old age.* New York: MacMillan.

Horley, J. 1984. Life satisfaction, happiness and morale: Two problems with the use of subjective well-being indicators. *The Gerontologist* 24:124-127.

House, J., and Robbins, C. 1983. Age, psychosocial stress, and health. In M.W. Retey, B.B. Hess, & K. Bond (Eds.), *Aging in Society: Selected reviews of recent research* (pp175-197). Hillsdale, NJ: Eribaum.

Howe, C.Z. 1987. Selected social gerontology theories and older adult leisure involvement: a review of the literature. *The Journal of Applied Gerontology* 6:448-463.

Hoyt, D., and Creech, J. 1983. The Life Satisfaction Index: a methodological and theoretical critique. *Journal of Gerontology* 38(1):111-116.

Hurh, W.M. and Kim, K.C. 1984. *Korean immigrants in America: A structural analysis of ethnic confinement and adhesive adaptation*. Cranbury, NJ: Associate University Press.

Hurh, W.M., Kim, H.D., and Kim, D.C. 1978. *Assimilation patterns of immigration in the US: A case study of Korean immigrants in the Chicago area*. Washington, D.C: The University Press of America.

Jackson, J.S. 1989. Race, ethnicity, and psychological theory and research. *Journal of Gerontology* 44:1-2.

Jackson, J.S., Chatters, L., and Neighbors, H.W. 1986. The subjective life quality of Black Americans. In F. Andrews (Ed.), *Research on the quality of life* (pp. 193-213). Ann Arbor: University of Michigan, Institute for Social Research.

Jones, E.E., and Kurchin, S.J. 1982. Minority Mental Health. New York: Praeger.

Kastenbaum, R.J. 1977. A "should" that has become an "is". *International Journal of Aging and Human Development* 7(4): 281.

Kendis, R. J. 1980. The elderly Japanese in America: an analysis of their adaptation to aging. *Dissertation Abstracts International* 41: 07A.

Kapadia, K.M. 1986. *Marriage and family in India*. London: Oxford University Press.

Kiefer, C., Kim, S., and Choi, K. 1985. Adjustment problems of Korean American elderly. *Gerontologist* 25(5): 477- 482.

Knapp, M.R. 1976. Predicting the dimensions of life satisfaction. *Journal of Gerontology* 31(5): 594-604.

Koh, S.D., Sakauye, K., Koh, T.H., and Liu, W.T. 1984. *Relocation and acculturation stresses in Asian Indian immigrants*. Chicago: Pacific/Asian American Mental Health Research Center (unpublished).

Kohen, J.A. 1983. Old but not alone: informal social supports among the elderly by marital status and sex. *The Gerontologist* 23: 57-63.

Kuo, W. H., and Tsai, Y. 1986. Social networking, hardiness, and immigrant's mental health. *Journal of, Health and Social Behavior* 27: 1333-149.

Kutner, B., Fanshel, D., Togo, A., and Langner, T. 1956. *Five hundred over sixty: A community survey of aging*. New York: Russell Sage Foundation.

Larson, R. 1978. Thirty years of research on the subjective well-being of older Americans. *Journal of Gerontology* 33:109-124.

Lawrence, R. H., and Liang, J. 1988. Structural integration of the Affect Balance Scale and Life Satisfaction Index A: Race, Sex and Age differences. *Psychology and aging* 3: 375-384.

Lawton, M. P. 1972. The dimension of moral. In D. Kent, R. Kastenbaum, & S. Sherwood (Eds.), *Research, planning and action for the elderly*. New York: Behavioral publications.

Lawton, M. and Cohen, J. 1974. The generality of housing impact on the well-being of older people. *Journal of Gerontology* 29:194-204.

Lee, J. 1991. *Asian American experience in the United States*. North Carolina: McFarland & Company Inc. Publishers.

Lemon, B., Bengtson, V., and Peterson, J. 1972. An exploration of the activity theory of aging: Activity types and life satisfaction among in-movers to a retirement community. *Journal of Gerontology* 27:511- 523.

Leonard, W.M. 1981. Successful aging: An elaboration of social and psychological factors. *International Journal of Aging and Human Development* 14: 223-232.

Liang, J., and Fairchild, T.J. 1979. Relative deprivation and perception of financial adequacy among the aged. *Journal of Gerontology* 34: 756-759.

Liang, J., Dvorkin, L., Kahana, E., and Mazian, F. (1980). Social integration and morale: a re-examination. *Journal of Gerontology* 35: 746-757.

Liang, J. 1982. Sex differences in life satisfaction among the Elderly. *Journal of Gerontology* 37(1): 100- 108.

Liang, J. 1985. A structural integration of the Affect Balance Scale and the Life Satisfaction Index A. *Journal of Gerontology* 40:552-561.

Liu, W.T., Yu, E.S., Chang, C, and Fernandez, M. 1990. The mental health of Asian American teenagers: a research challenge. In Arlene R. Stiffman and Larry E. Davis (Eds.), *Ethnic issues in adolescent mental health*. Newbury Park: Sage.

Lohmann, N. 1977. Correlations of Life Satistfaction, Morale and Adjustment Measures. *Journal of Gerontology* 32(1): 73-75.

Lowenthal, M.F. 1964. *Lives in distress: The paths of the elderly to the psychiatric world*. New York: Basic Books.

Lowenthal, M.F., and Haven, C. 1968. Interaction and adaptation: intimacy as a critical variable. *American Sociological Review* 33(1): 20-30.

Maddox, G., and Campbell, R.T. 1985. Scope, concepts and methods in the study of aging. In R.H. Binstock & E. Shanas (Eds.), *Handbook of aging and the social sciences, pp 3-31*. New York: Van Nostrand Reinhold.

Maddox, G., and Wiley, J. 1976. Scope, concepts, and methods in the study of aging. In R. Binstock and E. Shanas (Eds.), *Handbook of aging and the social sciences*. New York: Van Nostrand Reinholt.

Maguire, G. 1981. An exploratory study of the relationship of valued activities to the life satisfaction of elderly persons. *The Occupational Therapy Journal of Research* 3:164-172.

Markides, K.S. 1979. Predicting self-rated health among the aged. *Research on Aging* 3:97-112.

Markides, K.S., and Martin, H.W. 1979. A causal model of life satisfaction among the elderly. *Journal of Gerontology* 34:86-93.

Mancini, J.A., Quinn, W., Gavigan, M.A., and Franklin, B. 1980. Social network interaction among older adults: Implications for life satisfaction. *Human relations* 33:543-554.

Medley, M. L. 1976. Satisfaction with Life among persons sixty-five years and older. *Journal of Gerontology* 31(4): 448-455.

Medley, M. L. 1980. Life satisfaction across four stages of adult life. *International Journal of Aging and Human Development* 11: 193-209.

Melendy, H.B. 1977. *Asians in America: Filipinos, Koreans, and East Indians*. Boston: Twayne Publishers.

Motwani, J. K. 1986. An exploration of the activity theory of optimal aging in India: a cross-cultural perspective. *Dissertation Abstracts International*, 47:10A.

Murphy, H. 1977. Migration, culture and mental health. *Psychological Medicine* 7:677-684.

Nanny, R. 1982. Uprooting and surviving, an overview. In R. Nann (Ed.), *Uprooting and Surviving*. Boston: D. Reidel Publishing.

Negron, C.V. 1987. Retirement: A comparative study of retirees from professional and non-professional level occupations in a higher education setting. *Dissertation Abstracts International* 48:2447. (University Microfilms No. 8724223)

Neugarten, B., Havighurst, R., and Tobin, S. 1961. The measurement of life satisfaction. *Journal of Gerontology* 16:134-143.

Neugarten, B.L. 1964. Summary and implications. In B.L. Neugarten & Associates (Eds.), *Personality in middle and late life*. New York: Atherton.

Neugarten, B.L. 1968. The awareness of middle age. In B.L. Neugarten (Ed.), *Middle age and aging* (pp. 93-98). Chicago: University of Chicago.

Neugarten, B. L. 1976. Grow old along with me! The best is yet to be. In S. White (Ed.), *Human Development in today's world* (pp. 134-145). Boston: Little Brown.

New, K., Henderson, J., and Padgett, D. 1985. Aging, ethnicity, and the public: policy implications. *Journal of Applied Gerontology* 4(1):1-5.

Palmore, E., and Luikart, C. 1972. Health and social factors related to life satisfaction. *Journal of Health & Social behavior* 13: 68-80.

Palmore, E. 1981. *Social patterns in normal aging: findings from the Duke Longitudinal Study*. Durham: North Carolina, Duke University Press.

Pihlbad, C., and Adams, D. 1972. Widowhood, social participation and life satisfaction. *Aging and human development* 3:323-330.

Quinn, W.H. 1980. *Relationships of older parents and a recursive model of a theory of interaction and their effects on psychological well-being of the aged*. Unpublished doctoral dissertation, Virginia Polytechnic Institute and State University.

Rao, V., and Rao, N. 1981. Determinants of life satisfaction among Black elderly. *International Journal of Aging & Human Development* 14(1):55-65.

Reinhardt, J.P. 1988. Kinship versus friendship: social adaptation in married and widowed elderly women. *Dissertation Abstracts International*, 49: 1410. (University Microfilms No. 8809482).

Rhodes, A.A. 1980. The correlates of life satisfaction in a sample of older Americans from a rural area. *Dissertation Abstracts International*, 41: 1958. (University Microfilms No. 8026072)

Riley, M. W., and Foner, A. 1968. *Aging and Society Inventory of Research Findings*. New York: Russel Foundation.

Robinson, J., and Shaver, P. 1969. *Measures of social psychological attitudes*. Survey research Center, Ann Arbor: University of Michigan.

Ross, A.D. 1970. *The Hindu family in its urban setting*. Toronto: University of Toronto Press.

Salamon, M.J. 1988. Clinical use of the Life Satisfaction in the Elderly Scale. *Clinical Gerontologist* 8(1): 45-54.

Sells, 1968. *The definition and measurement of mental health.* Washington, D.C: U.S. Government Printing Office.

Sharma, G. C., and Tiwari, G. 1983. Gerontology: viewpoint of Hindu psychology. *Perspectives in Psychological Research* 6(1):19-24.

Shebani, B.L. 1984. Correlates of life satisfaction among older Libyans and Americans. *Dissertation Abstracts International* 45:2812. (University Microfilms No. 8429271).

Sheth, M. 1995. Asian Indian Americans. In *Asian American* (P.G. Min, Ed.), pp169-198. Thousand Oaks, CA: Sage Publications.

Sikri, A. 1989, August 11. When the old are far from home. *India Abroad*, pp. 1, 12-14.

Skolgund, P.A. 1986. An assessment of life satisfaction and depression in community elderly and their relationship to other demographic and social variables. *Dissertation Abstracts International* 47:2030. (University Microfilms No. 8618999)

Sluzki, C. 1979. Migration and family conflict. *Family process* 18:379-390.

Snow, R., and Crapo, L. 1982. Emotional bondedness, subjective well-being, and health in elderly medical patients. *Journal of Gerontology* 37: 609-615.

Spradley, J. 1980. *The ethnographic interview.* New York: Holt, Rinehart, and Winston.

Spreitzer, E., and Snyder, E. 1974. Correlates of life satisfaction among the aged. *Journal of Gerontology* 29: 458-464.

Stock, W.A., Okun, M.A., and Benin, A. 1986. Structure of subjective well-being among the elderly. *Psychology and aging* 1:91-102.

Stoller, E.P., and Earl, L.L. 1983. Help with activities of everyday life: Sources of support for the noninstitutionalized elderly. *The Gerontologist* 23:64-70.

Stones, M.J., and Kozma, A. 1980. Issues relating to the usage and conceptualization of mental health constructs employed by gerontologists. *International Journal of Aging and Human Development* 11:269-281.

Streib, G. F, and Schneider, C. J. 1971. *Retirement in American society: Impact and process.* Ithaca, NY: Cornell University Press.

Streib, G. F., and Thompson, W. E. 1960. The older person in a family context. In C. Tibbitts (Ed.), *Handbook of Social Gerontology* (pp. 447-488). Chicago: University of Chicago Press.

Stumpf, N.E. 1982. The relationship of life satisfaction and self-concept to time experience in older women. *Dissertation Abstracts International* 43: 3924. (University Microfilms No. 8307700)

Sue, S., and Morishima, J. 1982. *The mental health of Asian Americans*. San Fransisco: Jossey-Bass.

Suh, H. 1987. The relationships among life satisfaction, locus of control, and death anxiety as perceived by Korean and American older adults using selected personal demographic variables. *Dissertation Abstracts International, 49*, 320. (University Microfilms No. 8804112)

Thomas, L.E., and Chambers, K.O. 1989. Phenomenology of Life Satisfaction among elderly men: quantitative and qualitative views. *Psychology and Aging* 4:284-289.

Thompson, G. 1973. Work versus leisure roles: an investigation of morale among employed and retired men. *Journal of Gerontology* 28:339-344.

Thompson, G., Streib, G., and Kosa, J. 1960. The effects of retirement on personal adjustment: a panel analysis. *Journal of Gerontology* 15:165-169.

Tilak, S. 1989. *Religion and Aging in the Indian tradition*. New York: SUNY Press.

Tobin, S., and Neugarten, B. 1961. Life satisfaction and social interaction in the aging. *Journal of Gerontology* 16: 344-346.

Toledo, S.T. 1982. Housing satisfaction, supportive services, and social networks as related to life satisfaction of the elderly. *Dissertation Abstracts International* 44: 689. (University Microfilms No. 8315730)

Toseland, R., and Rasch, J. 1979. Correlates of life satisfaction: An AID analysis. *International Journal of Aging and Human Development* 10: 203-211.

Tsukahira, Y. 1988. Reaching out to families of the Asian elderly. *Aging* 358: 11-13.

Usui, W.M., Keil, T.J., and Durig, K.R. (1985). Socioeconomic comparisons and life satisfaction of elderly adults. *Journal of Gerontology* 40: 110-114.

U.S. Bureau of the Census. 1989. We, the Americans: We, the Asian and Pacific Islanders. *Current population reports* ASI:89(2326-1.15). Washington, D.C: U.S. Government Printing Office.

U.S. Bureau of the Census. 1990. Census of population, supplementary reports. *Detailed ancestry groups for states.* (1990 CP S-1-2). Washington, D.C: U.S. Government Printing Office.

U.S. Bureau of the Census. 1991. Profile of the foreign born population in the United States. *Current population reports* ASI:91 (2546-2:162). Washington, D.C: U.S. Government Printing Office.

U.S. Bureau of the Census. 1993. *1990 census of population, Asians and Pacific Islanders in the United States* (CP-1-1). Washington, D.C: U.S. Government Printing Office.

U.S. Department of Commerce, Bureau of the Census 1981. *1980 Census of the Population, General Population Characteristics.* Washington, D.C: U.S. Government Printing Office.

Vatuk, S. 1980. Withdrawal and disengagement as a cultural response to aging in India. In C. Ferry (Ed.), *Aging in culture and society*, 126-148. New York: Praeger.

Walsh, E.M. 1986. Volunteerism among the elderly: A secondary analysis of a national survey. *Dissertation Abstracts International* 48: 483. (University Microfilms No. 8701902).

Watson, G. 1930. Happiness among adult students of education. *Journal of Educational Psychology* 21: 1.

Ward, R., Sherman, S., and LaGory, M. 1984. Subjective Network Assessments and Subjective Well-Being. *Journal of Gerontology* 39(1): 93-101.

Ward, R.A. 1985. Informal networks and well-being in later life: A research agenda. *The Gerontologist* 25:55-61.

Weinberger, M., Darnell, J.C., Martz, B.L., Hiner, S.L., Neil, P.C., and Tierney, W.M. 1986. The effects of positive and negative life changes on the self-reported health status of elderly adults. *Journal of Gerontology* 41:114-119.

Willits, F.K., and Crider, D.M. 1988. Health rating and life satisfaction in the later middle years. *Journal of Gerontology* 43: 172-176.

Wolk, S., and Kurtz, J. 1975. Continued growth and life satisfaction. *Gerontologist* 15:129-131.

Wolk, S., and Telleen, S. 1976. Psychological and Social Correlates of Life Satisfaction as a function of residential constraint. *Journal of Gerontology* 31(1):89-98.

Wylie, M. (1970). Life satisfaction as a program impact criterion. *Journal of Gerontology*, *25*, 36-40.

Index